Leap into Literacy

Teaching the tough stuff so it sticks!

KATHLEEN GOULD LUNDY

Pembroke Publishers Limited

© 2007 Pembroke Publishers
538 Hood Road
Markham, Ontario, Canada L3R 3K9
www.pembrokepublishers.com

Distributed in the U.S. by Stenhouse Publishers
480 Congress Street
Portland, ME 04101-3400
www.stenhouse.com

We acknowledge the financial support of the Government of Canada through the Book Publishing Industry Development Program (BPIDP) for our publishing activities.

We acknowledge the assistance of the OMDC Book Fund, an initiative of the Ontario Media Development Corporation.

Library and Archives Canada Cataloguing in Publication

Lundy, Kathleen Gould
  Leap into literacy : teaching the tough stuff so it sticks / Kathleen Gould Lundy.

Includes index.
ISBN 13: 978-1-55138-212-8
ISBN 10: 1-55138-212-1

1. Effective teaching.   2. Active learning.   I. Title.

LB1027.L85 2007   371.102   C2006-906376-1

Editor: Kate Revington
Cover design: John Zehethofer
Typesetting: Jay Tee Graphics

Printed and bound in Canada
9 8 7 6 5 4 3 2 1

Contents

Appendixes

Introduction: Expanding the Space of Possibles

If children can't learn the way we teach, maybe we should teach the way they learn.
—Ignacio Estrada

Leap into Literacy encourages you to envision your classroom as a place of infinite possibilities—where inspired planning provides key entry points for different kinds of learners and where teaching responds to student needs, digressing if it has to. It also encourages you to differentiate instructional practices to meet the needs of all your students.

You may find that you need a sense of permission to look at the span of readiness in your classroom and to experiment with different approaches to effective literacy instruction. You may also need to remember the central role that imagination can play in learning—where students are given time to remember past events, imagine new realities, and brainstorm innovative solutions to problems that might affect their lives. I hope that this book will provide you with the encouragement necessary to try the approaches advocated here.

Leap into Literacy is about teaching "hard" skills in what some would call "soft" ways—by engaging students in active, experiential learning with material that matters to them. As Regina Pally writes in *The Mind–Brain Relationship*, the brain learns best when it "does" rather than when it "absorbs." The ideas presented here are formulated around research that affirms learning environments must be active, challenging, safe, and relevant and that all students need time to construct personal understandings about difficult concepts and powerful ideas. *Leap into Literacy* recognizes that when students are given choice and ongoing mentorship, encouragement by others, time to talk themselves into understanding, and the opportunity to approach a text or a task in a variety of ways, they can master skills, learn information, and become critically aware of their own possibilities as learners.

In a speech to the Council of Drama in Education, Jonothan Neelands described how we, as teachers, can unlock the many kinds of possibilities to be found in our students. Many students think they are who they have been *told* they are and their sense of the "possibles" of others may be limited as well—not based on personal experience, but on stereotypes and hearsay. Neelands sees the self as "a space of possibles."

> And what we need to do … is to help kids to expand that space of possibles. So the space of possibles of self include a confident self, a powerful self, a leader self, an achiever self. But at the same time, the space of possibles of the other begins to expand so that I understand that those kids who look different from me come in as many different shapes and sizes and forms as I do, or we do. In that way I can begin to imagine myself as the other and I can begin to imagine the other in myself. And if we can expand those

boundaries out it will be an important way of us feeling comfortable about difference whilst at the same time being able to recognize what is human in each other.

The strategies and ideas in this book help take students beyond those boundaries.

Awaken a Questioning Attitude

We are interested in education here, not in schooling. We are interested in openings, in unexplored possibilities, not in the predictable or the quantifiable, not in what is thought of as social control. For us, education signifies an initiation into new ways of seeing, hearing, feeling, moving. It signifies the nurture of a special kind of reflectiveness and expressiveness, a reaching out for meanings, a learning to learn.
—Maxine Greene

Underpinning this book is a belief in the important role that teachers have in a democratic society: to awaken in our students a questioning attitude towards their own lives and the world around them. Teaching is a learned skill that relies upon the collective knowledge and values held in the classroom—the knowledge that the teachers and the students bring to topics and the value that they assign to the topics being studied. The resources teachers choose will reflect their knowledge and values.

Information is important to education, but how we teach students to manage and interpret this information is the centre of the teaching/learning dynamic. Because of the emphasis on the "right answer approach," students often begin to think that there must be incorrect and correct answers to *all* questions. But life is not like that.

Ambiguity and different perspectives need to be taken into account to gain the full picture of an incident, a person's life, a relationship, an action, a statement, or an account. Critical thought is required to decipher the meaning behind the words, and asking difficult questions often helps us gain understanding into complex situations. Most compelling questions produce multiple solutions and new insights.

Remember, Words Can Create Worlds

Literacy is the most important weapon in the arsenal that the poor, the dispossessed, the unprivileged can use to transform themselves and the societies that marginalize them.
—Jonothan Neelands

In our rush to make students literate, we sometimes forget why we value literacy so much. In the excitement, energy, and turbulence of the classroom, we need to remember why we are striving so consistently towards this goal of literacy for all.

First, we need to remember that *language is how thought is made* so what we think about—our relationships with one another, the problems we encounter, our future possibilities, the complexities of the world—all our thoughts are connected to how literate we are. Words are important. They help us articulate our future and lead us to a more enlightened understanding of what we are and what we can do to help one another to survive.

Second, literacy is connected to social responsibility because literate citizens read all sorts of texts critically, listen intently to others without passing immediate judgment, are aware of their feelings and empathetic to the needs of human beings, have the capacity to write for multiple audiences in a variety of ways, and can speak coherently and skillfully in public. Literate citizens are enlightened citizens. They can live with ambiguity, think about multiple points of view, critically analyze what they are learning so that they can make educated judgments about taking actions that are in the best interest of all.

Third, critical literacy is essential because words have the power to create worlds. Susannah Heschel, daughter of the famous rabbi who did such important work during the American civil rights movement, passes on what her father told her about words: "Words are themselves sacred, God's tool for creating the universe, and our tools for bringing holiness—or evil—into the world. He used to remind us that the Holocaust did not begin with the building of crematoria, and Hitler did not come to power with tanks and guns; it all began with the uttering of evil words, with defamation, with language and propaganda. Words create worlds, he use to tell me when I was a child. They must be used very carefully. Some words, once having been uttered, gain eternity and can never be withdrawn. The book of Proverbs reminds us, he wrote, that death and life are in the power of the tongue."

Lay Out the Possibilities

The task of the excellent teacher is to stimulate "apparently ordinary" people to unusual effort. The tough problem is not in identifying winners; it is in making winners out of ordinary people.
—K. Patricia Ross

All teachers aim to have an impact on their students' lives and to guide them into safe harbors of understanding. Often, however, the waters can be rough as we face huge challenges in terms of our students' learning styles, attitudes, intelligences, needs, interests and backgrounds. Many of us find that some of our students have already "shut down" by the time that they enter our classrooms and have come to look upon school as a place of personal failure. For all sorts of reasons, they have spent lots of time learning how to cope rather than learning how to learn. Their discouragement and feelings of inadequacy are not only huge hurdles for them, but for us as well—their teachers and the people who love them and want them to be successful in school and in life. All teachers need to believe that they can turn their students' discouragement and feelings of failure around—that they can reacquaint their students with their power as learners as they lay out the possibilities, both internal and external, that will ensure their success.

How we begin to turn fear of failure and disappointment around is partially dependent on our willingness to try new things—to rethink how and what we are teaching and to honestly look at what techniques are working and what are not. We need to find ways to link the material to what students already know, to dig deeply into our teaching bag of techniques to find ways of revealing our students' personal connections to the material they need to learn. We must rely on our capacity to intrigue, to inspire, and to arrest the attention of our students. We must be open to the possibility of debate, personal narratives, and different viewpoints coming together to encourage interest.

Help Students Construct Their Own Understanding

I am interested in classroom activities that help students construct their own understanding. I want to see students grappling with problems that interest them, reading texts orally with others, representing their new understandings in drama and movement, visual arts, and electronic media, sharing leadership in groups, talking through ideas, all the time actively engaged in material that contains ideas that force them to rethink what they know and reframe their understanding about how the world works. I want to see students doing, thinking, talking, writing, making connections, and representing their understanding in words and in art forms. Equally important is hearing students reflect on how, what, and why they are learning in various subjects.

David Merrill, who supports a more behavioral approach to instruction, discusses the basic assumptions that constructivists subscribe to in a 1991 *Educational Technology* article, "Constructivism and Instructional Design." I have outlined these ideas here.

- *Learning is constructed.* People learn from experience. It is a process in which one builds an " ... internal representation of the world" (p. 46).
- *Interpretation is personal.* Reality is not shared. What a person learns is based on a personal interpretation of experiences. (Many constructivists would agree that people build their own interpretations of the world, but not necessarily that they live in their own separate realities.)
- *Learning is active.* The learner takes an active role in developing knowledge through experience.
- *Learning is collaborative.* Conceptual growth comes from interacting with others and sharing multiple perspectives. Through sharing perspectives, people change their "internal representations" (p. 46).
- *Learning is situated.* Learning should be placed in situations meaningful to students and relevant to the context in which the new information will be used. Real-world contexts are valuable, but not essential—imagined contexts can be created in a classroom through drama and simulation. Anchored and situated learning strategies are preferred.
- *Testing is integrated.* Testing should not be a separate activity, but integrated with the learning experience.

The activities in this book use the collective imagination of students to solve problems so that everyone is working towards finding possible solutions and grasping new ideas. As they work with different kinds of texts through discussion, drawing, moving, writing, and other forms of representation, students refine their ideas. Their work fuels more investigation.

All these activities address in some way concerns about literacy, safe schools, social justice, and character education. All learners can enjoy the activities, but they are designed specifically for those students who crave and need active, imaginative, open-ended approaches. Before introducing the activities, help is provided in setting up classrooms where everyone's story is honored and acknowledged—an important step in ensuring that students feel safe to become engaged in what they are learning on many different levels: physically, intellectually, and emotionally.

Teaching is a matter of awakening and empowering today's young people to name, to reflect, to imagine, and to act with more and more concrete responsibility in an increasingly multifarious world. At once, it is a matter of enabling them to remain in touch with dread and desire, with the smell of lilacs and the taste of a peach. The light may be uncertain and flickering; but teachers in their lives and works have the remarkable capacity to make it shine in all sorts of corners and, perhaps, to move newcomers to join with others and transform.
—Maxine Greene

In this book, you will be introduced to proven strategies that engage students in literacy activities. Students work with texts in a hands-on manner and often find themselves "inside" the stories, poetry, and other kinds of material, interpreting events, becoming characters, questioning relationships, refining their ideas, mining words, phrases, and larger texts for meanings, patterns, and personal connections, and subsequently achieving fresh understandings. As students work from entry points that intrigue them to culminating tasks that allow them to discover that they are learners with lots to contribute in classrooms and beyond, they will, without realizing it, "leap into literacy."

The Challenges of Promoting Active Learning

I have encouraged teachers to do this kind of work for years as they work towards balanced literacy classrooms. I have helped them find the time in a crowded curriculum to engage with "teachable moments" in more active, experiential, and inclusive ways so that they reach more of their students and have happier and more exciting classrooms.

It hasn't been easy to convince board officials, principals, and teachers about this kind of approach. Time is one of the issues. Belief in this kind of learning is another. As curriculum demands have become more specific and less imaginative, it has been more difficult to convince teachers of the inherent rewards of active learning. For me, there have been many moments of discouragement and frustration.

I will always remember listening to a radio interview with Ursula Franklin on the evening of September 11, 2001—the day of the tragic events in New York City and Washington. Ursula Franklin, internationally renowned social scientist, mathematician, and peace advocate, was talking to a CBC journalist about how discouraged she had become about peace education. She said she felt that she had been "spectacularly unsuccessful" at advocating for peace throughout the world. "But," she said, "just because I have been 'spectacularly unsuccessful' does not mean that I am going to give up the fight for a fairer, more just, and peaceful world."

I feel the same way. I have no worries about inculcating new and independent thinking among students, and I work daily with parents, teachers, student teachers, faculty, administrators, and students who are grappling with issues of human diversity. Although aware of the nostalgia among some teachers for a time of more obedience and regimentation, I am convinced of the connection between education and full citizenship; I remain intent on enlivening students' thinking by encouraging authentic and powerful experiences to happen in classrooms.

Learning—The Only Thing That Never Fails

If we take the time and the risks to make changes in our teaching, I know that classroom work can be more active, exciting, relevant, imaginative, and enjoyable. I know that students who construct their own understanding through personal engagement learn more and think more. I know that if we did more of this kind of teaching, we would have fewer behavior management issues in classrooms, fewer dropouts, more parental interest, and less failure.

Granted, it is challenging to do this kind of work: it is student-centred and teachers must open up the conversation in their classrooms so that they can listen to the fragments of understanding and go from there. If you work this way, your classroom will be noisier. The work will sometimes be exhausting. But I can promise that you will never be bored and you will be constantly fascinated by what is going to happen next.

As T. H. White writes in *The Once and Future King*:

"The best thing for being sad," replied Merlin, beginning to puff and blow, "is to learn something. That's the only thing that never fails. You may grow old and trembling in your anatomies, you may lie awake at night listening to the disorder of your veins, you may miss your only love, you may see the world about you devastated by evil lunatics, or know your honour trampled in the sewers of baser minds. There is only one thing for it then—to learn. Learn why the world wags and what wags it. That is the only thing which the mind can never exhaust, never alienate, never be tortured by, never fear or distrust, and never dream of regretting. Learning is the only thing for you. Look what a lot of things there are to learn."

There are lots of things to learn—and myriad ways to teach. What follows are suggestions for active, imaginative, differentiated literacy instruction.

1. Lay the Groundwork

All of us are intent on nurturing a sense of excitement and anticipation about learning in our classrooms. Many of us spend hours envisioning experiences both in the classroom and beyond that will engage students in complex, multi-layered learning. I try very hard to structure opportunities for students to learn actively so that they will talk together about the texts they are reading, make choices about how to represent their new knowledge, present various viewpoints, and debate issues. If they engage with material that has meaning to them, they find it easier to research new information, jot down notes, talk and plan together, sketch out ideas about characters, design sets for stories, imagine different perspectives and realities, and create new understandings with their peers. In the process of working with partners and in small and large groups on authentic tasks, they gain the skills and knowledge required to communicate what they are learning.

Help Students Choose Success

Perhaps the most important choice that students make each year is their choice to be as successful as possible. For students who have failed at many things, their decision to move ahead and overcome hurdles will present challenges. Scaffolding the work, providing peer mentors, scheduling student meetings, and allowing students to work from their strengths initially are strategies to keep in mind.

One of my most profound experiences as a teacher took place many years ago. A secondary school English and Drama teacher, I was promoted to a half-time drama adviser to the Toronto Board of Education. My first assignment was to be part of a research project that involved Grade 1 students in story drama activities. I was one of two drama people who visited four inner-city elementary schools three times every two weeks for five months to teach drama to six-year-olds. I learned a lot about drama in those months and had the wonderful opportunity to watch Doris Brook at Queen Victoria teach her students how to read and write. I saw huge progress and was impressed by Doris's high expectations and her belief that her students would be reading and writing by the end of Grade 1.

I remember asking Doris why her students were all so successful and remember her saying: "The trick is to make them choose to be successful. If they think that this is what is supposed to happen and they are taught well, they just fall into reading and writing because I tell them from the very beginning that they are going to be able to do this."

Doris's attitude had a real impact on me and every morning I returned to teach in my school with the same attitude. My belief in my Grade 9 English students and our tireless work together allowed me to see them as competent readers and writers, and they began to see themselves that way as well.

Offer Choices That Lead to Challenge

Beyond making students believe in themselves, it is important to give students choices about the activities they are going to do and the methods by which they will accomplish the goals that have been set out for them. Choice allows for negotiation, ownership, and student accountability. You need to structure your classes to enable students to pursue, deepen, and expand their interests while at the same time moving into realms in which they are less comfortable. Students need to be aware of the path that lies ahead, to learn to challenge themselves to do more than what they know they are good at.

I try to offer my students choices that will lead them into realms of challenge and responsibility. Gradually, I move them out of their comfort zones so that they begin to do more complex, demanding tasks in incremental steps.

I often give students choices about the different ways to represent their learning. I encourage them to tell their "learning story" in multiple ways using a variety of techniques and media. In this way, students learn important presentational skills. They own their new understandings, know what they know, and feel confident about teaching others.

- *Offer choice in what to read:* graphic novels, short story anthologies, novels, poetry, newspapers, magazines, comics, computer texts, and how-to books.
- *Offer choice in how to respond to a text:* collages, board games, poetry cafés (see Chapter 4), talk-show interviews, dance, character analyses, photo shoots, tableaux (see Chapter 7), hot-seating (see Chapter 8), prepared improvisations, scripts, storyboards, diary entries, writing in role (see Chapter 8), and artifacts (see Chapter 9).
- *On occasion, offer choice in partners and group members:* Group work should be part of the daily experience of students. The constellations in the groups should vary and students should have opportunities to work with everyone in the class as a partner and as a member of a group, so that relationships grow. If you begin the year with short group activities that do not put a lot of stress on the relationships, you will be surprised by the friendships fostered. The most important thing is to state clearly your expectations that everyone will work with everyone throughout the year and students should reach out to those who are not their friends. Although choice is important, ensure that the English Language Learner (ELL) students are spread evenly around the room and that strong leaders are separated. Be sure to monitor and give extra support to socially challenged students.

Assess for Student Success

Assessment can help students leap into literacy. As teachers, we aim to provide students with tools that help them understand how they learn best and strategies that they can employ to learn better.

One thing to be aware of is the limitations of various assessment techniques. For instance, multiple choice and fill-in-the-blank types of assessments are not effective for monitoring anything but factual knowledge; they could be used for reading comprehension. Performance task assessment—where students demonstrate what they have learned through a culminating task—requires more time and negotiation with students, but gives more information about what students are learning on many different levels.

Students have a big role to play in the assessment process. Involving them in assessment causes assessment to become a form of instruction (see the personal assessment tools in the Appendixes). Students need to monitor their own progress by setting goals and understanding the processes they can use to attain those goals. They need to understand

- what they are doing;
- why they are doing it;
- how to tell if they are doing it well; and
- what they can do to achieve further success at the task.

The teacher's job is not to judge a student's work quickly, but to focus on assessment for learning as well as on assessment of learning; provide targeted feedback on performance, including clear indications of how to improve; and concentrate on the performance rather than the student. When I set up active, engaging activities, I monitor skills and comprehension. For instance, if I have a class do Role on the Wall (see Chapter 7), the activity gives me all sorts of information about the vocabulary my students know and have learned. As students defend their choices of words or phrases, I can assess their levels of understanding and thinking.

It is vital to identify what you want to know about your students' learning: that governs the type of assessment task you should choose. A summary of assessment task types appears below. It is loosely based on Bloom's taxonomy, which I have found helpful in framing assessment tasks.

- If you want students to demonstrate what they **know**, have them identify, underline, match, label, name, or find.
- If you want students to **analyze** what they are learning, have them compare, contrast, classify, take apart, chart, or survey.
- If you want students to give you a sense of what they **comprehend**, have them retell, give examples, paraphrase, summarize, infer, or interpret.
- If you want students to **synthesize** all of the information, have them predict, build, imagine, invent, modify, or suppose.
- If you want students to **apply** what they are learning, have them use, demonstrate, report, dramatize, put together, or collect.
- If you want students to **critically evaluate** what they are learning, have them recommend, debate, defend, rank, judge, or criticize.

Face the Space

The kinds of activities that I describe in this book require space to be found and negotiated. In using the phrase "Face the Space," I acknowledge the challenge of this problem, but argue that it can usually be resolved. Often, teachers decide against active learning in their classrooms because they feel they lack access to space in their schools. My Hong Kong pre-service teacher candidates often tell me that what I am proposing could never happen in Hong Kong schools because of the space requirements.

There are, however, many ways to think about classroom space:

- Students, if working in partners, can work in between the desks.
- Students can put four or five desks in a circle for group work.
- The creation of a large rectangle of desks allows face-to-face class discussions and a large space in the centre of the classroom for active, up-on-your-feet work.
- Students can move the desks to the side of the room (as quietly as possible) and leave a circle of chairs for everyone to sit on.

These configurations are not ideal, but can work if the students are interested in and challenged by the texts and activities presented to them. The only one who wishes for more space is usually the teacher. Students are likely to be delighted about interacting in a different group configuration and about working together to find the meaning in texts.

Of course, you can work with your principal and various staff members, such as the librarian, to get space:

- Libraries are usually wonderful, but there can be interruptions and schedule restraints.
- Gyms are prone to acoustical problems, but there are ways of dealing with this. Have your students sit in the corner and face you so that they can hear your initial instructions. Once the students are up on their feet and working in groups, use a tambourine or a drum as a control device. At the beginning, you might practise by saying something like, "When I hit the drum, I want you to 'freeze' and listen to further instructions."

You may also find forgotten spaces that are used for storage or hallways that are not used very often—these can have real potential for interactive learning.

I encourage my pre-service teacher candidates to think about space carefully when planning their lessons. I ask them to consider how they can use space efficiently so that disruptions are minimized and students can focus on the task at hand. If the task is co-operative, then the students should be facing one another; if the students are to respond individually, then they need to be isolated from one another so that they are not tempted to talk and can concentrate on their individual work.

Here are ways to address this last concern:

- Each student sits back to back with a partner.
- The students move their desks so that they are on their own.
- The students find their own spaces in the room away from others.

Set the Mood

Mood is important when you are working in active ways to bring texts to life and then communicate those responses to the class as the audience. Music enhances mood. Lighting sustains it.

I often turn off some or all of the classroom lights to create a different feeling in the room. After I do that, I aim the light of an overhead projector on the ceiling so that the light is somewhat diffused; then, I play appropriate music to set a new kind of atmosphere in the room. I choose recorded music carefully because it can be a potent stimulus for storytelling, Role on the Wall (see Chapter 7), drawing, moving, and writing in or out of role. Sometimes, the students request that the music be played at other times in the lesson because they have enjoyed it so much.

When I worked with a team of artists, teachers, and consultants creating the Drama/Dance Project at Winchester Public School, we were faced with a dilemma: the discrepancy between morning and afternoon rehearsal settings. The two visiting classes spent half of the day working in a professional dance studio in the Canadian Children's Dance Theatre (CCDT) with mirrors, a sprung floor, change rooms, and even a live accompanist. For the other half of the day, they worked in a small portable near the playground of the junior school.

The portable was standard fare, but creative ideas turned the room into another kind of studio. Deborah Lundmark, the artistic director of the CCDT, graciously allowed us to borrow the fine red rug normally placed in the entryway of the theatre. Cleaned and placed in a strategic part of the portable, the rug became a space where the drama artists invited students to sit, talk, listen to stories, and so forth. The other item that helped set a more compatible mood was a stand-up lamp that Lorraine Sutherns, the co-ordinator of the project, brought from home. The lamp lit the ceiling of the portable so that when the overhead lights were turned off, it set just the right atmosphere in which to think, wonder, remember, dream, improvise, and listen.

The kinds of music and lighting effects that you use in the classroom can enhance the experience of learning for students. Often, they find the changed atmosphere magical; the different mood alters their perceptions of the environment and of themselves as learners. They become more generous with one another, more relaxed, and more willing to imagine and dream together. New thoughts happen in new spaces.

Come to the Same Page

I ask myself questions all the time: "As I plan this lesson or unit, how am I going to move the students beyond superficial understandings to new insights about the way in which the world works? How am I going to begin? Where will I stand? How will I group them effectively? Should I dim the lights so that there is a certain kind of mood in the class? What do I have to do to literally get the students on the same page—excited and motivated to learn?"

In my experience, creating a context for learning matters. I help my teacher candidate students at York University find compelling narratives, redesign their classroom spaces, and ask probing, open-ended questions so that they can give their students authentic reasons to think, read, write, and speak in public to audiences that care about what they are saying. Students become motivated when they find that they have authentic reasons for doing the hard work in school.

One of the most exciting planning sessions that I became involved with concerned putting together a Grade 7 unit on the geography of Canada. My teacher candidate students were trying to find a way to begin. I asked them to think of the great stories that bind our country together. What are we most proud of? What defines us as a nation? We initially talked about the building of the railroad and the near loss of Quebec during the last referendum, but we soon hit upon the story of Terry Fox. In Canada, Terry is an icon that everyone knows. Students are connected in many ways to the Terry Fox story because many take part in or help organize an annual fund-raising run.

We decided to look at the geography of Canada through the eyes of Terry Fox. Our goal was to link this emotionally charged, inspirational story to the geographical details of our country.

We asked ourselves many questions: After Terry dipped his toe into the Atlantic Ocean off the shores of Newfoundland and began to run on his one good leg across the country—what was his experience like? What did he see? Where did he sleep? What did he eat? What cities did he visit? What kind of music did he listen to on the radio? What was the weather like? What kind of temperatures and weather systems did he have to endure as he journeyed across this enormous land?

And as Terry became more famous, as his courageous and painful journey was reported more and more in the media, who did he meet? What special sightseeing places was he taken to? When he fell asleep at night after his journey, what landmarks would he remember? What special people would he see in his dreams?

And when he was re-diagnosed with cancer in Thunder Bay, Ontario, and was unable to continue, what did Terry miss? What great landmarks along the Trans-Canada Highway did he never see? What people did he not get the chance to meet? What geographical challenges did he not face?

I knew we had it. The story of Terry Fox so easily provides an entry point for students to learn about Canada. Terry's story is emotional and inspiring and, by creating imaginative tasks that let students enter into the story, the geography facts and figures become important to learn. (See Chapter 10 for more information on this unit.)

Imaginative use of space, an array of student choices, and the establishment of an intriguing classroom atmosphere woven into learning contexts that have personal relevance all play their part in laying the groundwork for dynamic teaching and learning. When students find themselves in intriguing spaces where they have a measure of choice, when they feel supported by their teacher and peers, and when they realize that they are going to learn about people, places, ideas, and relationships to which they have personal connections, the road to becoming literate becomes easier and more enjoyable.

2. Greet the Group

Every human being is driven to search for meaning. We all try to create patterns from our environment and we all learn to some extent through interaction with others. Because ours is a social brain, it's important to build authentic relationships in the classroom and beyond.
—Geoffrey Caine

The ways that we organize classroom life should seek to make children feel significant and cared about—by the teacher and by each other. Unless students feel emotionally and physically safe, they won't share real thoughts and feelings.
—Linda Christiansen

I encourage my student teachers to think clearly about the kind of relationship that they want to establish with their students. We want to be their teachers and not their friends, but we want the lines of communication to be open enough so that we are aware of their interests, their triumphs, the challenges they face in each learning situation, and the gifts they bring to our classrooms in terms of academics, energy, sense of humor, and generosity of spirit. Dorothy Heathcote, who has influenced me greatly, encourages all teachers to approach any teaching situation with this idea: "I do not demand this of you. The task at hand is of such significance that it demands it of *us.*"

The ways in which class members interact with one another and with you affect the literacy achievements of all. No students are going to use their public voices in the classroom if they feel shy, under attack, or misunderstood. Shy students or ELL students are not going to read out loud and take risks in writing and speaking if they do not trust the group and their acceptance in it.

We need to establish a firm, safe foundation so that students willingly, and with excitement, "leap into literacy." The ground must be solid, but flexible, allowing a spring to every step taken. The footing should be secure, but permit students to soar easily into the air. Students need to feel safe about experimenting, trying out new ideas, and voicing their opinions. They will do all of this in a supportive environment: one where many "spotters" help them journey further into literacy.

Let All Voices Be Heard

I have often been criticized for the time I spend establishing group cohesiveness in my classrooms. For the most part, I carry on because I know that if students learn one another's names, find out about their histories and present interests, and talk about their common goals, the classroom will be a safer haven for all voices to be heard. Peers can reinforce one another's responses, extend one another's visions, and challenge one another's positions. This give-and-take interaction can happen only in classrooms where emotional and intellectual safety has been given credence.

Good teachers know that complex learning is enhanced when challenges are interesting and threat is diminished. In order to have a successful literacy program, there needs to be an acceptance of everyone's ideas and an ethic of hearing everyone's voice. If people are open to others' ideas and patient about their tentativeness, kids will begin to risk saying what they think: they will feel confident that they will not be laughed at or put down in any way.

Students come to class not only to read and write, but also to clarify their thoughts and work towards new understandings of difficult knowledge. As students learn to interact competently in their classrooms, they gain confidence to interact with larger communities and experts in the field. They learn first by testing themselves with their peers.

Build Scaffolding

True learning involves figuring out how to use what you already know in order to go beyond what you already think.
—Jerome Bruner

Part of making a classroom safer for your students is to provide scaffolding for students who are slower to grasp ideas and learn strategies. Scaffolding, as Jerome Bruner uses the word, refers to the support, guidance, and instruction provided by the teacher or knowledgeable peers to help students move from where they are in their understanding to a higher level. The zone of proximal development theory, developed by Lev Vygotsky, states that students learn through expert guidance given by the teacher and the students in the class. Confident teachers rely on those students who have easily learned various concepts to provide support to their peers. Students can provide their peers with models of accomplishment and can demonstrate how they learned a certain concept or worked through a problem.

Scaffolding is not limited to human interaction. Teachers can use computer programs to help students with a learning difficulty. In every case, learners become more aware of the strategies that are available to them. Once the students have learned the strategy, they can use it to their advantage when they are faced with a problem.

Teach Group Process Skills

The most powerful survival principle of life is diversity. As David Suzuki writes in *Sacred Balance: Rediscovering Our Place in Nature*, there is no single right way that works—there will be hundreds or thousands. The reason that we ask students to work in groups stems from the belief that a variety of ideas pooled together produces better products. This is true if negotiation is part of the process and everyone has a voice in what is decided by the group. To achieve this, competition must be diminished and collaboration established and nurtured. The class needs to accept the importance of teamwork in establishing a classroom environment in which every student feels respected and has responsibility as a group member.

By the time students reach Grade 3 or 4, they have had both good and bad experiences of working in groups. They are aware that group work can be fraught with competition, domination, exclusion, and unfairness. Some students, imagining that they will be forced out or dominated by other group members, shut down before they even begin. Others remain determined to work only with those students whom they know are responsible and will pull their weight. Sometimes, a group goal is achieved by only a few of the members, and disappointment and resentment linger in the classroom. Goals are achieved, but often the group breaks apart in the process. Sometimes, the group fails to achieve anything.

The problem is that we tend to ask students to work in groups without teaching them how to do so. Just as students need to be equipped with information about how to become effective readers and writers, they need to be taught group process skills so that they can achieve together. Students need to learn how to work co-operatively and productively with their peers. They need to become aware of how groups function, the different ways that groups can reach a decision, what kinds of behavior people manifest in groups, and what other roles and responsibilities group members might consider to make the groups that they find themselves in function better. We need to teach students group process skills that will help them work with a wide range of people throughout their lives.

There are many ways to teach about group interaction. I try to make it simple so that students enjoy learning about how groups function. They will also begin to be aware of how important it is to share the influence in a group and experience the satisfaction that comes with everyone being part of a task's successful completion.

"Group decision-making is one of the most significant aspects of group functioning," affirm David and Frank Johnson in *Joining Together* (p. 62). Kids need to be taught that the best way to work in groups is to strive for a consensus so that most members are comfortable with the decisions. Often, kids average the opinions or take a vote so that a decision is made quickly, but neither of these ways makes everyone feel they have a stake in what happens. To reach consensus, group members must be able to voice an opinion and to be heard. They must also be willing to let go of some of what they want.

Essentially, an effective group does two things:

1. It achieves its goal, which must be something of significance.
2. It supports itself so that the working relationships among the group members do not falter and all agreed-upon tasks are carried out.

It is important that group members are aware of these two things as they work. At the end of each working session, I ask my students these three questions:

- Is the group getting closer to achieving its goal?
- Is the group maintaining itself so that everyone feels like a contributing and valued member?
- What is it you are doing to make these two things happen?

Your role as teacher is to constantly check in and find out how things are going. You are interested in the task, but also interested in how they are doing as group members. You might hand out the checklist "How We Work as a Group," as I do, and have students fill it out individually. "Making the Group Work," which provides possible text for a group work poster, lists what students should be striving to do. (See page 23.)

How We Work as a Group

Group Members: _____

_____

- ❏ We are clear about the task.
- ❏ We have agreed to work together.
- ❏ We are listening to one another.
- ❏ We are trying not to interrupt one another.
- ❏ We are including everyone in the discussion.
- ❏ We are making sure that we stay on task.
- ❏ We are taking short breaks when we need them.
- ❏ We are dividing up the work.
- ❏ We are following through.
- ❏ We are working from our strengths.
- ❏ We are monitoring the process.
- ❏ We are teaching one another about what we know.
- ❏ We have agreed on the roles and responsibilities of each group member for this assignment.
- ❏ We are determined to finish the task and to remain a cohesive group.

Help Students Become Aware of How They Work in Group

Making the Group Work

Work from your strengths.
Monitor the process.
Create timelines and tasks.
Support one another.
Make sure that everyone is involved.
Take time to build the group.
Share the leadership.
Allow everyone to play a significant part.

One way that I help students become aware of group roles and responsibilities is to have them reflect on how they think they work in groups. I have them fill out a sheet about their understanding of group process. Sometimes, I have them work with a partner to do this exercise to allow students to talk about their experiences before they write about them.

- Describe a group experience that you found very positive.
- Why do you think the group functioned well?
- Describe a group experience that was not successful.
- What do you think that the group did not do so well?
- Are you someone who likes to work in a group? Why?
- What strengths do you bring to the group?
- What weaknesses do you have in a group setting?
- How do you behave if the group functioning begins to break down?
- What kinds of new roles would you like to try?

These questions appear as a reproducible page for students in the Appendixes.

Observing the Group: I have students "practise" group process during group assignments, such as brainstorming or interpreting text for a Readers Theatre presentation. I choose two people to work together and have them observe the group and give feedback to the members. The students I choose are diplomatic and sensitive, and try to be positive and encouraging. They focus on three different members and consider these questions for each one:

- How much and in what manner did they contribute to the group?
- How well did they listen to the ideas of others?
- How often did they ask for the opinions and ideas of others in the group?

Monitoring Interruptions: One way to promote group work is to have students do a problem-solving activity while the observers record the number of times the students interrupt. Interruption is often a healthy part of communication, but sometimes it is helpful for students to be aware of how some of them dominate group work and make other people feel uncomfortable because of this.

Often, students are unaware of how they function in groups. They are quite happy to get feedback as long as it is given in a kind and diplomatic way. Students are usually interested in how they are perceived and the information that they receive informs the work that they do in other groups on other projects. I ask the students to reflect on their work in groups and set goals for themselves that they can work towards the next time.

Keep these sorts of group roles in mind.

A reproducible page, "Assessment of Work Done in Groups," appears as an appendix.

Goal-oriented Roles	Support-oriented Roles
initiator	encourager
questioner	active listener
source of new ideas	tension reliever
summarizer	mediator
researcher	compromiser
goal setter	standard setter
co-ordinator	checker of emotions
evaluator	communication assistant

Create Connections

If space is an issue, involve students in dealing with it as a problem-solving situation. Chapter 1 provides a reminder of basic layout alternatives in a regular classroom.

In classrooms where active exploration happens regularly, an enjoyable atmosphere is essential to student success.

Games are a really good way to set up learning communities where everyone feels connected and classrooms become places of friendship, care, and conscience. They can help students come to feel safe expressing their views and ideas.

The word "game," however, often evokes images of a competition in which someone wins and many lose. Winners feel good because they perceive themselves to be quicker, smarter, or stronger than others; losers may feel badly if they perceive that their loss is a personal failure. Unhealthy attitudes towards competitive games do not create group cohesion, mutual acceptance, and trust—exactly what is needed for students to flourish in classrooms.

On the other hand, *co-operative* games are an excellent way to set up learning communities where everyone feels connected and students strive to achieve a common goal. Participants learn to be aware of how to include all the students in the class and help everyone achieve success. Co-operative games forge friendships and connections that eventually allow classrooms to become "communities of conscience." People become aware of who is involved, who has shut down, who is being excluded, and who is becoming more confident.

How do games fit into literacy classrooms?

There needs to be a commitment on the part of everyone—not just the teacher—to be patient as students find their public voices. To write for an audience and to speak about one's ideas requires an empathetic and encouraging environment. In collaborative classrooms, students feel safe to express their views and ideas. Co-operative games promote a feeling of goodwill because everyone achieves. Because of positive group feelings, people begin to be more open to ideas and more patient about shyness and tentativeness. If students know that they won't be laughed at or put down, they try harder and may take risks.

Games can be challenging to set up in terms of control, but the rewards are great. You might say, "When I hit the tambourine and call 'freeze,' stop in time and motion and listen to further instructions." Have your students help you figure out how to make the games work better, be fairer, and be more challenging to all. In my experience, students have creative ideas and love it when the group implements them!

Co-operative Games in the Literacy Classroom

Stomp It: Ask the students stand in a circle. One person begins to stomp with both feet (left and then right). The person to his/her right does the same thing and the "stomp" is passed around the circle. Have the students pass the stomp more quickly, and then with their eyes closed.

Clap It: Have students remain standing in the circle and join the circle yourself. Make eye contact with the person to your left. Clap your hands. The person on your left responds to the clap by clapping back, turns to the person on her or his left, establishes eye contact, and claps once. That person claps back and then "passes the applause" to the person on his or her left. The applause is passed around the circle until it comes back to you. It is really important for the students to maintain eye contact as they pass the applause.

Encourage the exercise to go quickly and watch the electricity in the room. More than one clap can be sent around the circle. Listen to suggestions from the students about how the exercise could be changed or adapted.

Name It: Ask the students to stand in a circle. Have them say their names one at a time and do an action. Have the rest of the class repeat the person's name and the action. Continue around the circle until everyone has had a turn. Tell the students that they do not have to plan the action. They should try to do it as spontaneously as possible.

Play the game again but in a number of different ways. Have the students say their names in an overly dramatic way, loudly, or in a whisper. Direct them to make actions that are squiggly, straight, or robot-like. The rest of the class can mimic the name and motion.

Change It *or* **Pass the Pencil:** Ask the students to form groups of five or six and sit in circles. Produce a pencil and demonstrate how that pencil can be transformed into something else by miming various actions using it. For instance, the pencil can become a toothbrush, a violin bow, or a hockey stick. Explain that you are going to give each group a pencil. The person who receives it is to pass it to the student to the right who will be expected to change the pencil into something that it is not. As the student does the action, the rest of the students can call out what the object is. If someone cannot think of an idea, he or she can pass the pencil on to the next person. ELL students can mime an object that they want the name for and the rest of the class can help them out by telling them what the word is.

Three Changes: Have the students find a partner and decide who is *A* and who is *B*. Ask the *A*s to face the *B*s so that the class is divided into two lines. Prompt the *A*s to take a good look at the *B*s and observe as much as they can about their physical appearance. Then instruct the *A*s to turn around. While the *A*s are not watching, the *B*s change three things about their appearance, for example, removing an earring, changing the cuff on a pant leg, or putting hair behind ears. Have the *A*s turn around and guess what three things were changed. After a short time of guessing, the *B*s can tell their partners about those changes that were missed. Switch roles so that the *A*s get a turn making changes, too.

Back to Back/Face to Face: Have each student find a partner and tell partners to stand back just far enough away not to be touching each other. Have them change their position as you call out different commands, such as "Face to face," "Shoulder to shoulder," "Elbow to elbow," or "Elbow to shoulder." When you say, "Change partners!" the students find other partners and the commands begin again. Encourage students to find as many partners as possible and if new to one another, to learn their names in the split second of the meeting.

Line Up in Order Of …: Have the students arrange themselves in two equal groups facing each other in a straight line. One line is Team X and the other is Team Y. Each team will work together silently as quickly as its members can. On your signal, have them arrange themselves in order of height, tallest people at one end and shortest people at the other. Then have the students arrange themselves in order of their birthday month. They say their birthdays out loud with all team members paying attention.

After this part of the game, ask the students if they heard any birthdays to which they relate in some way. (Examples: My sister has the same birthday as Linda; Ahmed and I have the same birthday and we never knew that last year.)

Finally, have the students line up in alphabetical order based on first names. Ask them to say their names out loud so that everyone can hear the names and the way that they should be pronounced. (I play this game when I am a guest in classrooms—it lets me hear how students want their names pronounced. I take special care not to mispronounce names and embarrass students.)

Atom: Have the students "walk to the empty spaces in the room" without bumping into one another. Tell them to walk quickly, change direction, walk on tiptoes, walk backwards, walk sideways, and so on. On a signal, such as a tambourine tap or drum beat, have them freeze in time and motion. Congratulate them and tell them to relax.

Advise them that they are going to repeat the activity, but this time you will say something like "Atom 3!" They are to act as if they are atoms and join up with the students who are closest to them to form a group of three. If they don't already know each other, they must learn one another's names quickly. They are then to walk throughout the room again. If you say "Atom 5!" they are to form a group of five. If anyone is left over—a common phenomenon—groups are to hide those people in their constellations. For example, if there are 31 students and you say, "Atom 5," there will be six groups of five with one person left over. Go around the classroom and check to see the "extra people" hidden in the group. You might also make calls such as "Atom 2 + 3" or "Atom 7 – 2." Keep the groups moving and changing quickly until everyone has been jumbled up.

The Seat on My Right Is Free: Have the students sit in a circle on chairs. Make sure that there is one empty chair. The person to the left of the chair says, "The seat on my right is free. I would like to invite [someone in the class] to sit beside me." The person who is invited crosses the circle, which frees up a chair. The game continues with the person to the left of the empty chair repeating: "The seat on my right is free, I would like _____ to sit beside me." Make the rule that everyone receives an invitation and that no person can be invited more than once.

Name Switch Now: Students stand in a circle. One person is "It." "It" establishes eye contact with someone across the circle and then says his/her name and the name of the other person. "It" begins to walk towards this person, who establishes eye contact with another, says his/her name and the name of the other, and begins walking towards that person. They switch places. The game should be played quickly and everyone should have a turn. Encourage students to "give each other their eyes" as they say their names and somebody else's.

Heigh Ho: Have students sit in a circle. Appoint someone to be "It." "It" stands in the middle of the circle and says, "Everyone who is wearing sandals, change places." Everyone has to move to another chair. "It" runs to a chair and sits down. The person left standing then becomes "It." "It" can then say something else like, "Everyone who watched TV last night, change places!" or "Everyone who wishes it was still summer vacation, change places!" If the person who is "It" says, "Heigh Ho," everyone must change places. Play the game quickly.

Strength Bombardment: Get students into groups of five sitting on chairs. Have them number themselves off 1-2-3-4-5. Hand them each a card. The stu-

Before playing Strength Bombardment, it may be a wise idea to talk about the importance of building up people's self-esteem and how that contributes to students' efforts to work well together in groups.

It is helpful for teachers to ask themselves these questions: Why am I playing this game? What new skills will my students learn from it?

dents should focus on the members of their group and write down five things that they like about each person, for example, he has a good sense of humor, she is a good friend, he is an excellent ball player, or she always shares her lunch. There is to be no talking. On a signal, have the students stop writing and focus their attention on number 1. Their task is to quickly tell number 1 all of the things they wrote down about that person. Encourage them to "bombard" number 1 with all of his or her strengths. They then go on to the next person. Everyone should get many compliments. Debrief by asking students how the exercise made them feel individually. What could have made it work better?

Applying Games to Lesson Content

Games can provide a dynamic way into content.

In one memorable instance, a game played in a drama class was powerfully applied to course content. A group of pre-service teachers were creating an integrated unit using various sources to explore the topic of pandemic. The pre-service teachers involved the class in a classic game of Shake-hands Murder. In the original game, students are instructed to close their eyes and the teacher chooses someone to be "It." That person, the murderer, goes around the room shaking hands. If "It" squeezes the hand twice, it means that murder has been committed, and the students must die imaginative and ghastly deaths. In this particular game, however, the leader asked the class to close their eyes. She said that she was going to pick someone to be "It" and that person would go around the room and shake the hands of three people by squeezing twice. Those three people were then to go around and shake three more hands before they died. At the end of the game (which happened very quickly), every member of the class lay on the floor. The suggestion of how randomly and quickly a pandemic can infect a whole community hit home with a powerful impact.

It seems ironic to end the chapter promoting group cohesiveness by describing a game such as this; however, I want to make the point that when students are actively engaged in co-operative work, they are working in another realm—physically, emotionally, and intellectually. Excitement and electricity are in the room as they find themselves collaborating to make the games work. As they interact with one another and enjoy a few moments of laughter together, they begin to see one another in new ways.

In order for students to become literate—to read, write, and speak with fluency—they need an empathetic adult guiding, teaching, and encouraging them, but they also need the support of the class. My argument is that the whole class needs to be rooting for everyone in the classroom—the strong students as well as the weaker ones—so that everyone can leap into literacy, either from a place of tentativeness or from a place of eagerness, to find the surprise and joy that await them.

3. Scan Your Plan

The map is not the territory.
—Richard Courtney

Lesson planning and delivery are dynamic processes. They require imagination, a developed sense of timing, an understanding of the prior knowledge of students, information about how to make accommodations and modifications for those students who need them, careful consideration of space, experience in making transitions from one activity to the other, and creative management of materials. They also demand an excitement about the path ahead and a flexibility to change gears before and during the lesson. The goal is to make learning experiences as powerful and as transformational as possible.

Plan for Surprise

If teachers do use outcome tests and ability scores, and many will be required to do so, they should be aware that every expectation they hold of what a child can and cannot learn should be mistrusted. This means that they should make a hypothesis that they are willing to revise. If we give the learner particular opportunities and different learning conditions, he might prove the test's predictions to be wrong. Teachers should always be ready to be surprised by any child.
—Marie Clay

Successful teachers know that if they plan carefully and think things through not only from their vantage point, but from the perspectives of their students, they will be able to manage time, people, information, and resources efficiently, making the learning experience enjoyable, thought provoking, and effective. They also know that "the map is not the territory" and that what they have spent time planning can change once they encounter the students. Often, they have to switch gears quickly and think on their feet to make things work. They adjust the lesson to make things go more smoothly every moment that they are teaching.

As teachers, we also need to let ourselves be surprised by our students. I love Marie Clay's statement about being willing to revise our hypotheses about them. The ability to be surprised stems largely from withholding judgment for as long as possible. Many times when I work as a guest in classrooms without knowing the students, I place demands on them that their teachers might not. The teachers, as observers, are often surprised by the students' responses and their ability to achieve the goals set. Sometimes, students not earlier viewed as "bright" shine in unexpected ways.

Students need to see their classrooms as places where they can reinvent themselves. As they learn new things, meet new people, establish new relationships, and represent who they are through different media, they can change as people. They should see themselves as part of making the classroom work. Although students chart their own intellectual journeys, we, as teachers, set the course and help them along the way. Learning happens when student-knowledge and teacher-knowledge interconnect.

Successful teachers "scan the plan" before they begin and become adept at anticipating problems of space, time, groupings, resources, modifications, and accommodations so that the time spent teaching is efficient and enjoyable. Of course, all teachers make mistakes and sometimes realize too late that they should have done things, said things, remembered things … but if they note their mistakes, the next time they do the lesson, they will have a more successful experience. Adept reflective practitioners often think after a lesson, "These parts went well, but if I were to teach this lesson again I would remember to …"

In my more than 30 years of teaching students at all levels, I have found that I rely on my intuition when I work as a guest in a classroom, but also on fundamental classroom management strategies. Some of the ideas I implement are based on my understanding of theatre. For example, actors are told that they should never blame the audience. If something goes wrong when I am teaching, I take a constructive approach by reflecting on what I could have done or said that might have made the lesson work better. I don't dwell on the problems, but I do try to learn from them.

Twenty-five Tips for Classroom Management

How we set up classroom experiences is crucial to the success of our programs. The ways in which we negotiate for power and control when we first meet our students and when we work with them throughout the year will have a lasting effect. If power is given slowly to the students as they come to think of the work in the classroom as their own, any power struggles within a classroom can be minimized.

Teaching and classroom management are intertwined. How we set up a classroom and then manage the people, materials, space, and technology is all part of the teaching/learning dynamic. Classroom management is not separate from teaching, but part of the same experience.

Here are 25 simple classroom management tips that I have gleaned from my teaching. Some echo important ideas presented in Chapters 1 and 2. All reflect the need to anchor three attributes in our classrooms: security, affirmation, and control. You may find several tips that are new or especially useful to you.

1. Begin with high expectations for everyone in the room. Because I enter a classroom knowing that my lesson will change as soon as I meet the students, I try to remain hopeful and exuberant. By my manner, I let students know that I have high expectations for myself and that I expect their full attention to our task.

2. Allow for spontaneity. Treat your agenda as flexible and allow for spontaneous shifts in direction. Be prepared to negotiate. If the students see you as rigid and unwilling to discuss options and choices in the task before them, they sometimes shut down and get discouraged. You don't need to give away everything—but be prepared to listen to their suggestions.

3. Check how inclusive you are. Be as inclusive as possible. Check to see if you are asking for the same volunteers to answer questions or help you with work. Make sure that you look around the room and find the student whom you have not connected with in a while. Be sure to ask that person to help you.

As an excellent teacher, I must not be afraid to move out of my centre, and meet the children where *they* are.
—Dorothy Heathcote

4. Remember, it's not about you. In *Teaching to Transgress*, bell hooks writes, "teachers must be actively committed to a process of self-actualization that promotes their own well-being if they are to teach in a manner that empowers students" (p. 15). Students do not set out to ruin a lesson. Sometimes, things are going on in their lives that sap them of energy just when you need it. Try not to take student responses personally.

5. Let students know your plan. Give them an overview. Let them have some choice. Show them that you know what you are doing. Letting students in on the plan and offering an array of choices is often the best way to get them on your side. As you talk about the task or the project, show your enthusiasm and display your belief in their ability to do well.

6. Keep students at the centre. Try as much as possible to work with what students are giving you. Work from where they are—with their prior knowledge, with their capacity to work together, and with their enthusiasm for certain topics and ideas.

7. Be aware of students' developmental needs. Some things are just not going to work; some tasks are beyond your students' developmental stage. Revisit some of the literature on child and adolescent development. Perhaps, the task you have set is too abstract; perhaps, the requirements need to be adjusted.

8. Make rewards intrinsic. When some students are openly rewarded for good work, others feel disappointed and incompetent. If only some students receive tangible rewards, such as candy or an invitation to the pizza lunch, resentment from others in the class will fester and lead to some kinds of dysfunction. The reward should be the work itself.

9. Limit competition. Praise the group publicly, but praise and give individuals positive reinforcement privately. I find it works best to pull people aside and tell them how wonderful their work was rather than say it publicly. The same practice applies to criticism.

10. Don't wait to have everyone's attention before you begin. I used to wait, but now I begin on time. I focus on crafting as interesting a beginning to my lesson as possible so that students are sometimes intrigued, other times surprised, and will immediately settle down to listen and work.

11. Vary your groupings. Mix up the groups as much as you can so that students have opportunities to work with everyone in the room. Make sure you do individual, partner, small-group, and large-group work.

12. Distribute materials after the directions. If students are receiving materials, they are not listening. Talk first to get everyone's attention. When you feel that students have a moderate sense of what you are asking them to do or wanting them to know, hand out the materials they will need. There is always a flurry of activity. You may not have enough handouts or the handouts may get mixed up as they go around the classroom. So, distribute after you speak, maybe before you speak—but never during.

13. Stop, look, and listen. Listen carefully all the time to see who is on task, who is involved, and who has withdrawn from the conversation. I insist that my students listen to me. This simple, basic rule should be established at the beginning of the year: "When I talk, you don't."

14. Establish signals. You can dim the lights, hit a drum, use a chant … there are many possible signals. Having a signal that establishes silence quickly is crucial if you are going to do the kind of active, engaging work that I suggest. Ask for advice from your students about how you can make the signals work effectively.

15. Say "When I say go …." James Coulter, of the Toronto District School Board, taught me a great classroom management technique, "When I say go …." You say the phrase and then add the appropriate direction—you may pick up your pens, get into groups, hand out the materials, talk with one another. This simple phrase allows everyone to be ready to do what he or she has to do when they need to do it. It also reinforces that the teacher is the captain of the ship and keeps everyone safe and on task.

16. Face the space—organize the classroom seating. If students have to move desks aside to gain space to be active, negotiate with them ahead of time. "I am worried about the noise that we might make when we move the furniture. I don't want to disrupt other classes. Do you think that we could lift the desks and chairs to make the least amount of noise? It would also help if we did not talk as we move about. How else might we do this quickly, with minimal disruption?"

17. Make smooth transitions from one activity to another. If you have worked hard to establish a mood in the classroom by reading a story, you don't want to disrupt this mood by then getting the students into groups. A better idea is to get students into groups before you read the story. If you are worried that they won't pay attention, then insist that they sit facing only you; when the reading is finished, they can easily turn to their group members or partners.

18. Work the room. Once you have set the students their task, spend time with each group listening in on what they are saying, planning, and negotiating. Initially, you might take a few minutes to let them get on with what they are supposed to do, but your job is to be there for them—not overpowering them, but making suggestions, listening for and supporting their ideas, and monitoring the group process.

19. Modulate your voice. Voice modulation is an essential part of good teaching. When we read aloud to students, we modulate our voices to make the reading interesting. The same principle applies to directions. Sometimes, to get students' attention, it works to speak really softly; other times, to emphasize the importance of what they are learning, you might use a louder, more dramatic voice. Your voice can imbue the task with significance.

20. Take time to wait. I watch my student teachers make a great effort to master this as they learn how to teach. I struggle, too, with this important classroom management skill, often moving on before I should. I must stress, however, that when I have deliberately waited for students to think and to compose their thoughts before they answer, the effort has paid off. Timing is everything in teaching—go quickly some times, more slowly at others. As you gain experience, you will get it right.

21. Chunk information. This classroom management strategy is really important. We often give students too much information at one time. If we chunk it, students can digest the bits, act on them, and wait for more directions. Here is an example: (1) Make sure that you each have a pencil or a highlighter; (2) Get into your groups from yesterday and settle around a table; (3) In a few minutes, I am going to hand out a text that I would like you to read silently; (4) I am going to distribute it now; (5) You can begin reading when you receive it; (6) When you have finished reading the selection, I would like you to underline the words and phrases that you found interesting and want to know more about; (7) In your groups, discuss the words and phrases together. Consider these questions....; (8) Appoint a spokesperson to make jot notes on what you are saying; (9) In a few minutes, we will have a group discussion. Make sure that your spokesperson can summarize your group discussion; (10) Let's begin our class discussion.

22. Go group by group by group. I have a vivid memory of watching one of my student teachers with a Grade 4 class. The students had painted magnificent snow scenes that were piled carefully in the corner of the classroom. Not having gauged the excitement of the class, the student teacher told them to pick up their paintings. The students ran to the paintings and began grabbing some and accidentally tearing others. The host teacher intervened, but my student teacher was devastated. She learned a valuable lesson, though: to go group by group.

For beginning teachers, such experiences happen a lot. When planning your lesson, think these transition bits through and write notes about the best way to ensure that the lesson will run smoothly.

23. Stand by your student. I am often asked, "What do you do about the kid who is deliberately sabotaging the lesson?" It seems simple, but an effective strategy that nearly always works is to stand beside the student. Often, such students are seeking attention. By standing beside them as you give instructions and looking them in the eye, you take away some of their power in the classroom. Sometimes, I put my hand on the back of their chairs, too. I have used this technique for years, having learned it from a guidance workshop attended long ago.

24. Let students talk to partners. A few years ago, I watched R. H. Thomson conduct a workshop on Shakespeare with a Grade 11 class in an auditorium in a Toronto high school. He was working with another actor demonstrating techniques for uncovering the meaning in texts. The students were mesmerized by what he was doing and saying, but whenever he asked a question, there would be silence and embarrassment. On a break, the famous Canadian actor asked my advice for involving the students more, so I suggested my tried and true strategy—continuing to ask the questions, but having students talk to partners about the answers first. When the students have a chance to try their ideas out loud in this way, they gain more confidence about speaking in front of a group. Thomson adopted this approach, and the class became far more involved.

I also use this strategy when I have a class full of students with their hands up, all having something they want to contribute to the discussion. I stop and have the students talk to partners. They then have an opportunity to be heard and their frustration level diminishes.

25. End lessons artfully. There is never enough time to teach—but there should always be artistry to it. Beginnings should be intriguing, endings uplifting. If you work with these two ideas, you need to plan carefully and be organized. You might keep notes near you (as I do) to remind you of all of the organizational tasks that need to be done before the end of the lesson. These might include getting two volunteers to collect the response sheets, leaving 10 minutes at the end to put away the art materials and rearrange the desks for the next class and reviewing the assignment due next week and answering any questions that the students have. Get the organizational things done and leave time to reassemble the class as a group.

Take this time to build a community of learners. Give your students a collective pat on the back, nurture a vision of what lies ahead, and create excitement about what is to come. You can summarize what they have done so far, praise them for their efforts, or remind them of how they are going to apply this new learning to the next task. You could also read them a poem or a quotation that sends them on their way feeling good about themselves as learners. I do not always end my classes successfully—life in classrooms is often turbulent and filled with unexpected interruptions. I find, however, if I plan for closure that is unhurried and uplifting, the students remember what was said and we can start from there when we meet again.

Not all of these strategies will work all of the time, but they are worth implementing, especially as you get students up on their feet working with texts. As you work more and more in this way, your techniques will expand, and along with careful, but flexible planning, you will be better able to help your students make the leap into literacy.

4. Make Words Sing

Poetry: the best words in the best order.

—Samuel Taylor Coleridge

I want students to love words, be intrigued by them, and enjoy manipulating them to achieve new meanings and understandings. I want them to get excited by how words sound and to be aware of how writers place each word carefully on a page to achieve a desired effect. I also want them to see that meanings are often ambiguous and interpretations, many.

The activities in this chapter allow students to become more confident using language both orally and in writing. In an atmosphere of experimentation and joy, students can gain confidence working with different kinds of texts—discussing meaning and effect, and then manipulating words to achieve varying results. Some of these activities allow students to compose words in different formats; others ask that they use words to create new texts with different effects.

Work with Words That Resonate

We need to promote the student's recognition that language has a melody, that cadences count, that tropes matter, that metaphors mean.

—Elliot Eisner

One effective reading strategy I use in classrooms involves encouraging the students to find the line, word, or phrase that resonates for them. This activity can be done a number of ways with all kinds of texts, including poetry, scripts, monologues, descriptive writing, and letters.

I pass out the text and give the students a few minutes to read it silently; then, I read it to them. I want them to hear the text in its entirety and I can model the out loud reading for them. Sometimes, we read the text again as a whole class so that the students have an opportunity to "get their mouths around the words."

I then ask the students to stand up. I tell them that I am going to touch them on the shoulder, and when I do, they are to walk around the classroom reading the text out loud. They are to concentrate on reading the text and should not make eye contact with anyone. They must be careful not to bump into anyone or into the desks as they walk and read.

I define the space if I have to. If there are nooks and crannies in the classroom or spaces that I don't want them to enter, I tell them that at the beginning. I also tell them that when they get to the end of the story, poem, or excerpt, they are to return to the beginning of the text and read.

They walk and read for a few minutes. I read along with my students for this allows me to listen in informally to their oral reading without putting them on the spot. I make a mental note about those students who seem to be having difficulty and I gauge the oral reading facility of my ESL/ELL students.

Next, I ask them to "freeze" and prompt them to spend a moment finding the line, word, or phrase that captures their imagination or affects them in some way. It could be that they like the way that the words "spring off the page," that the image the line evokes for them is very dramatic, that the line is personally important, that this word is one of a very few they understand, or that they like the way the phrase sounds as they read it out loud.

I give the students a few minutes and then ask them to continue walking, saying that line out loud over and over. They thereby gain practice using their projected voices before the next part of the activity.

I ask everyone to freeze again. I tell them that when I touch them on the shoulder they are to say the word, line, or phrase out loud. They are to say it again if I indicate for them to do so. I play appropriate music softly and then we begin to create our own out-loud reading of the text.

Here is what a Grade 9 class in Brighton, Ontario, did with a poem called "The Sorrow of Sarajevo." On one side of the page is the original poem. On the other is a reading of the poem created by the students saying their favorite words, lines, or phrases randomly. They read their personal responses to the poem out loud projecting over the beautiful music of *Schindler's List*.

The Sorrow of Sarajevo is also the title of a book of eight poems by Goran Simic, translated into English by David Harsent and published by Cargo Press in 1996. Poems reprinted with permission of Goran Simic.

The Sorrow of Sarajevo By Goran Simic	**A Reading of "The Sorrow of Sarajevo"** By Goran Simic
The Sarajevo wind leafs through newspapers that are glued by blood to the street I pass with a loaf of bread under my arm. The river carries the corpse of a woman. As I run across the bridge with my canisters of water, I notice her wristwatch, still in place. Someone lobs a child's shoe into the furnace. Family photographs spill from the back of a garbage truck; they carry inscriptions: Love from … love from … love … There's no way of describing these things, not really. Each night I wake and stand by the window to watch my neighbour who stands by the window to watch the dark.	There's no way of describing these things not really not really blood to the street the corpse of a woman not really Someone lobs a child's shoe into the furnace Love from … love from … love … There's no way of describing these things not really I pass with a loaf of bread under my arm. Each night I wake Family photographs spill from the back of a garbage truck There's no way of describing these things not really not really Love from … love from … love … I notice her wristwatch, still in place Each night I wake and stand by the window to watch my neighbour love … who stands by the window to watch the dark love…. not really

I, as teacher, orchestrated the new reading, layering the words and images so that they worked dramatically.

Every time you do this exercise with a class, the outcome is different. You have to really listen to the response from each student and then weave together the voices and words to create a new poem of power and significance. I layer the responses, have students repeat lines, ask two different students to read the same line, and vary the length of the response from a phrase to a word to a sentence back to a word. As you get more experience doing this exercise, you gain the confidence to play with what your students are giving you. Usually, the impact of this exercise is powerful for all involved.

Clone the Poem

"Earth's Last Cry" is an example of the sort of relatively short, non-rhyming poem that I most recommend for this activity. An example of a student response appears to the right.

I always wanted a happy ending … Now I've learned, the hard way, that some poems don't rhyme, and some stories don't have a clear beginning, middle and end. Life is about not knowing, having to change, taking the moment and making the best of it without knowing what's going to happen next. Delicious ambiguity.

—Gilda Radner

"Earth's Last Cry" appears in *Rethinking Our Classrooms: Teaching for Equity and Justice* (Volume 2), published by Rethinking Schools.

Here is one way to help students focus on the meaning of a poem and encourage them to see how the form of a poem often dictates its meaning. Students work in partners. I give each pair an envelope that contains the individual lines of a

---

Earth's Last Cry
The earth
can't save the people.

Branches of willow
have no fingers
to pick up broken glass
from city streets.

Grains of sand
have no hearts
to pump oil out
of darkening water.

Blades of grass
have no knives
to cut away
thickening pollution.

Roots of trees
have no
feet
to trample
drug needles.
Petals of lilac
have no arms
to carry away
nuclear waste.

—Rachel M. Knudsen

A Cloned Poem
Petals of Lilac
Roots of trees
Grains of sand
Branches of willow
Blades of grass
Can't save the people.
Thickening pollution
Drug needles
Darkening water
Have no hearts
No feet
No arms
No fingers
To pump oil out
To pick up broken glass
To cut away thickening pollution
To carry
The earth
away

—Adapted by Josh and Henrie

poem cut into strips. Each pair finds a way to make the poem work in terms of its meaning. They do not need to use all of the lines and they may change verb tenses if they need to. They can cut away words, but cannot add new words. They practise reading the poem aloud and then share their version with another couple. Only after the students have compared the poetry and discussed their interpretations do I hand out the original poem.

Respond to and through Poetry

What's on the Line?: Sometimes I introduce poems that are missing the last stanza or the last couple of lines. I ask students to work in groups to write the missing lines. Each group presents the poem that they have worked with and then I present them with the original.

A Novel Response: When reading a novel with students, I ask that they keep a list of words that they did not earlier know, strong images that they have created in their minds as they were reading, and lines that they liked the sound of. In groups of five or six, they share their favorite words, images, and lines and learn from one another. Then, I ask them to create a five-line poem as a response to a chapter using everyone's ideas. They can rehearse a reading of the poem using everyone's voices in a variety of ways.

Often the poem triggers great discussions of the novel's meaning and students see the novel—the characters, the plot, and the landscape—with new eyes. Here is what a few students in a Grade 8 class created from the novel *Dust*, by Arthur Slade:

Yearning, knobby
A dark boot hit the ground, then another.
Windows black like empty eye sockets.
Noble pursuit, accelerated
Thunder needed clouds, didn't it?
—Sam, Nick, Athena, and Alex

A Grade 6 group sent this poem to me after I did this exercise with the introduction to *Julie and the Wolves*, by Jean Craighead George:

Earth buckles.
Not a tree grew anywhere to break the monotony of the gold-green plain.
Ponds and lakes freckle its immensity.
I never dreamed that I could get lost, Amaroq
Desperate predicament.
—Daniel, Tin, Seeko, and Maria

Five-Line Easy Readings: Poetry should be read out loud and celebrated, not just hung on the walls. When I create five-line poems with students, they work in groups and try reading the poems in different ways. The students have copies of the poems they have written or adapted in their hands. I usually have them copy their poems into their journals, where they become the "scripts" from which they work. Although the students are working in groups, I address them as a whole class and have them do the activities in their groups. Everyone is working in the same way—just with a different text.

My goal is for each group to come up with a unique way of reading their poem so I encourage them to explore as many ways of reading as possible. I do not want them to "set" the reading too soon. Here are some ideas to offer students:

- The group reads the poem in unison. Tell the students that when they get to the end of the poem, they should start reading it from the beginning again. They are to stop reading on a signal, such as a drumbeat.
- One person reads the poem. Prompt the group to listen to how the lines sound with a solo reader.
- The girls read the poem; the boys read the poem. Let students think about how the lines sound this way.
- Everyone reads a line each.
- Read every second word in the poem.
- Repeat certain words in the reading. Invite students to consider how this changes the meaning and sound of the poem. How would it work to have repetition of a word read by one group member throughout the reading?
- Introduce sound effects. Invite students to consider what happens when they use their voices to provide sound effects or make clapping and clicking sounds.
- Use pauses. Suggest that the students experiment with pausing before certain lines, words, or phrases. How does the silence change the meaning of the poem?
- Try reading the poem in a duet or as a trio. Consider what lines sound best this way.
- Find a way of standing in the classroom that will give the poem more significance. The students could group themselves in a tableau formation by a window and use the light in interesting ways. They could enter from the four corners of the classroom and stand in the centre. They could stand in a circle facing outwards. I find that if I provide a few suggestions to students, they quickly come up with ideas that are usually far more effective than mine.

Poetry is a way of taking life by the throat.
—Robert Frost

See Chapter 7 for more information on tableaux.

Poems for Two Voices

Poetry is beautiful shorthand.
—William Cole

Shadow poetry is written for two people to say out loud. The poetry usually has two columns—one for each person reading the poem. Each voice has some kind of relationship to the other voice, and the voices shadow one another in some sort of way. Sometimes, if two readers are to say something at the same time, the poet writes the words on the same line in each column. These poems often sound like a dialogue for two people. The sample below is not precisely a poem, but a student-generated script that could be made into a poem.

Meaning What?

"I wish ..."	"You wish what?"
"I wish that I could ..."	"That you could what?"
"I wish that I could find a way to ..."	"Find a way to what?"
"I wish that I could find a way to tell you ..."	

Paul Fleischman has written two anthologies of poetry for two voices: *I Am Phoenix*, a collection of poems about birds, and *Joyful Noise: Poems for Two Voices*.

Below is an example of a poem that lends itself especially well to this type of two-voice treatment. One way of setting it up for two voices is shown.

You Have Two Voices

The poem comes from *The Spirit of Canada: Canada's Story in Legends, Fiction, Poems and Songs*, edited and compiled by Barbara Hehner (Toronto: Malcolm Lester Books, 1999).

(A) You have
(A + B) two voices
(B) when you speak in English
(A) or your mother tongue.
(A+B) When you speak the way your people spoke
(B) the words
(A + B) don't hesitate
(B) but flow
(A) like rivers,
(B) like rapids,
(A+B) like oceans of sound,
(B) and your hands move like birds through the air.
(A) But then you take a stranger's voice
when you speak in your new tongue.
(B) Each word is a stone dropped in a pool.
(A) I watch the ripples and wait for more.
(B) You search in vain for other stones to throw
(A) They are heavy. (B) Your hands hang down.
(A + B) You have two voices when you speak;
(B) I have two ears for hearing.
Speak to me again in your mother tongue.
What does it matter how little I understand
(A) when the words pour out like music
(A + B) and your face glows like a flame?

—Nancy Prasad

Poetry is when words sing.
—Six-year-old boy

Soundscape Compositions

Christopher Logue writes, "Poetry cannot be defined, only experienced." In order for us to help students understand that poetry is more than words on a page, they need to experience the poetry with their voices, bodies, and hearts. Soundscapes are a wonderful way to introduce students to the power of poetry, to the nuance of words and phrases, to the art and design of the words and lines on the page.

Soundscapes are a combination of sounds related to a particular place or environment that are written down in a specific order and performed by a group. They are not sounds alone, but a combination of attitudes, feelings, memories, and associations, all related to a specific place. They can be composed by a group, and with much editing, can mimic the experience of being in a specific place at a specific time. Soundscapes, in other words, reveal the world in sound.

My Grade 12 students used to create amazing urban soundscapes of Toronto—the subway, the Gardiner Expressway at rush hour, the corner of Bloor and Yonge, alleys, walking the dog in the park. They would play with the words and make amazing sounds with their voices. They also added body percussion to their creation.

Here is how you can get your students to create soundscapes.

Generate titles for vocal soundscapes. Suggestions include Waking Up on a Hot Summer Day, Cities, Elevators, Drive-through Restaurants, Construction Sites, and School Cafeterias. In groups of four, students choose a title for their soundscape and then create appropriate vocal sounds for the images suggested by the titles. Have each group record their soundscape on a piece of paper. A sample appears below.

Invite your students to think of a soundscape as a sound chronicle—a collection of sounds in a temporal sequence that tells a story.

Soundscape: Restaurant Drive-Through on a Rainy Day

Sounds of window wipers—car coming to a stop, rain on the roof of the car, rolling down the car window

[radio] and now, a brand new hit …

Click. [Radio is turned off.]

May I take your order?
What do you want to order?
Huh?
What do you want?
Why did you turn the radio off?
Just tell me. What do …
Ahhh, man … I was listening to …
What do you want …? Hurry … HURRY.
Sounds of traffic, car horn, window wipers, and rain
I don't know.
May I take your order, please?
I'll have a …
Hurry.
Um … a …
Hurry
A Special combo 3
Make that 2 number 3s.
Anything to drink?
What?
To drink?

Click.
Don't turn that on …
Click.
But I was listening to …
That'll be $7.59. Please drive through. Window number one …
Sounds of gearshift, car moving, window wipers, traffic, rain

Prompt the groups to present their soundscapes to one other group each and to discuss their compositions. Then, have them exchange scores with other groups and perform one another's music.

You might invite students to bring in "found" instruments from home. These include egg beaters (non-electric), forks, and spoons. Working in groups, students experiment with all the sound sources they have collected to augment their soundscape.

Soundscapes Created from Novels and Plays

I sometimes stimulate the creation of a soundscape by having students work with and interpret excerpts from novels where the setting is as important as the characters. When teaching William Golding's *Lord of the Flies*, I had students create soundscapes from the following evocative paragraphs:

> Ralph grasped the idea and hit the shell with air from his diaphragm. Immediately the thing sounded. A deep, harsh note boomed under the palms, spread through the intricacies of the forest and echoed back from the pink granite of the mountain. Clouds of birds rose from the treetops, and something squealed and ran in the undergrowth. (p. 18)

> They were in the beginnings of the thick forest, plonking with weary feet on a track, when they heard the noises—squeakings—and the hard strike of hoofs on a path. As they pushed forward the squeaking increased till it became a frenzy. They found a piglet caught in a curtain of creepers, throwing itself and the elastic traces in all the madness of extreme terror. Its voice was thin, needle-sharp and insistent. The three boys rushed forward and Jack drew his knife again with a flourish. He raised his arm in the air. There came a pause—a hiatus—the pig continued to scream and the creepers to jerk, and the blade continued to flash at the end of a bony arm. The pause was only long enough for them to understand what an enormity the downward stroke would be. Then the piglet tore loose from the creepers and scurried into the undergrowth. They were left looking at each other and the place of terror. Jack's face was white under the freckles. He noticed that he still held the knife aloft and brought his arm down replacing the blade in the sheath. Then they all three laughed ashamedly and began to climb back to the track. (p. 33)

Another soundscape suggestion is to depict the storm in the opening scene of Shakespeare's *The Tempest*. Students could incorporate some of the lines of the scene into their soundscape. Consider the potential of these words.

A confused noise within: "Mercy on us!"—"We split, we split!"—"Farewell, my wife and children!"—"Farewell, brother!"—"We split, we split, we split!"

Antonio: Let's all sink wi' th' king.
Sebastian: Let's take leave of him. *Exit [with Antonio.]*
Gonzalo: Now would I give a thousand furlongs of sea for an acre of barren ground, long heath, brown furze, any thing. The wills above be done! but I would fain die a dry death. *Exit.*

The Poetry Café

Theme-based poetry units can have as their culminating task a poetry café to which parents and other members of the community are invited. Coffee and tea are served, and people are encouraged to bring their favorite poems. Students can write and perform their own poetry and add famous poems to the mix. Here are some suggestions to make your poetry café work:

- Have a theme (e.g., Schoolyard Blues, Our Community, Landscape Poetry, Family Poetry, Winter Time, or Spring into Verse).
- Present the poems in different ways—solo, choral reading, chanting, Readers Theatre, and Story Theatre (see Chapter 5).
- Use different genres (e.g., collective poems, such as "We are from …" [see Chapter 10]; students' own poems; the poems of others; famous/favorite lines interwoven to create new poetry; poetry in other languages; bilingual poems; poetry from many lands; sports poetry; and poetry accompanied by movement and music).

For one poetry café, my high-school students had live performances as well as videotapes showing poetry read in different locations in the school and in the neighborhood. We also invited audience members to choose favorite poems, rehearse them, and feel welcome to read them. The master of ceremonies welcomed everyone in rhyme. The event, held in the auditorium, began at 7 p.m. and ended at 9 p.m. Two parents read poems aloud.

I want my students to fall in love with language and begin to see how reading, writing, and speaking are all connected. I also want them to have the confidence to wield some control over what they are reading, discussing, or creating. I want them to become sensitive to the weight of words so that they attend to the meaning of other people's words. I hope that they will acquire the habit of reading intelligently and critically and will learn to say what they really mean. They need time and encouragement to mine words for meaning—to experiment with how texts sound out loud, how the words are organized on the page, how something said simply can be quite complex, and how meanings can be altered by minor changes.

Being able to work with language and confidently manipulate meaning gives us a certain amount of power over our lives. When we understand how words work, we have the assurance to use our critical faculties to think in new ways.

Students advertised the poetry café over the school public address system with this rehearsed ditty:
Poetry that is famous; poetry that is true
Poetry that has made us shed a tear or two.
Poetry that we have written, poetry that we have read
Come and listen, all of you, before you go to bed.

5. Stage the Page

Reading is asking questions of printed text. And reading with comprehension becomes a matter of getting your questions answered.

—Frank Smith

Reading is a process that relies upon the reader connecting in a personal way with the text and interacting with it. Reading is never static—it is a transaction between the text and what the reader knows and understands. This chapter provides many opportunities for students to interact with text and to work in groups while doing so. The ideas here are designed to increase vocabulary, comprehension, and critical thinking. As well, students become more fluent and confident in their reading and speaking capabilities. In groups, they read aloud after negotiating the meaning of the text with one another. They are in the active mode—bringing a text to life to be listened to, sharing the reading, feeling the sound in a poem, and experimenting with meaning. They are "making meaning" as they read in groups—envisioning, visualizing, experimenting with voice, and at the same time thinking about ways that the spoken words of text can affect listeners.

The Plea to Read

I love it when kids make the "plea to read." By this I mean that I am delighted when they wish that there was time to finish a story, when they want to read a line out loud again, but with a different attitude or emotion, when they do a first-time read-aloud of what they have written to appreciative peers, when they feel satisfaction because they have mastered difficult material and are ready for more. It makes the tough part of teaching worthwhile.

How many times have we relied on reading to students to calm them down, retrieve them from silliness, or bring a new world to their attention? As students get older, they still need to be read to: to have an experienced reader bring them into a world of fantasy and fiction. When I taught secondary school English I tried, not always successfully, to read to my students every day. They loved the time in the lesson when they could listen to a story, article, or poem and not have to respond in any way but as active listeners. Occasionally, a student would ask to read something to the class, and if the reading had been rehearsed, I would agree. I remember those times as magical moments.

Chants and All That Jazz

In order to help students get interested in reading out loud, I begin with jazz chants. Jazz chants are short, snappy poems and rhymes that can be said with a swinging rhythm—similar to rap or rapping. Students may perform these jazzy poems in small or large groups using their voices in different combinations to create meaning. I encourage them to use rhythm instruments to enhance the beat, if desired. Bilingual or ELL students need reading practice for fluency and pronunciation. Doing jazz chants provides these opportunities as the students must read and reread the material for final group performance.

An additional benefit of jazz chanting is that the students have the chance to develop a sense of the rhythm of the English language and to obtain practice using idiomatic phrases and expressions. Several kinds of jazz chants can be found in Carolyn Graham's books, such as *Jazz Chants* and *Let's Chant, Let's Sing…*

Be sure to use chants in your reading program. Reading chants out loud takes the pressure off the individual reader and the relaxed atmosphere encourages less fluent students to vocalize words that they ordinarily would not attempt.

- Begin by having the whole class read the jazz chant in unison. Here is a brief example:

    Who put the overalls in Mrs. Murphy's Chowder?
    Nobody answered. So, she said it all the louder!

- Have students vary the reading of the chant by changing the tempo: they could read it quickly, slowly, as robots, as babies, as soap opera actors, as detectives.
- Encourage students to use gestures.
- Then have them read alternate lines—you read one line and the class reads the next. You can then split the class in two, and ask one-half of the class to read one line and the other half of the class to respond.
- Read the lines alternately again, this time with lots of emotion. Vary emotions, for example, one side is anxious, while the other side does not care.
- Have half the students repeat the first phrase three times and the other group repeat the first sentence three times in answer. With the example above, it would go like this:

    Who put the overalls
    Who put the overalls
    Who put the overalls in Mrs. Murphy's Chowder?
    Nobody answered.
    Nobody answered.
    Nobody answered. So, she said it all the louder!

The following poem exemplifies the features of a good chant. It has great rhythm and emotion. It tells a story that we can relate to and each line brings strong images to mind. The poem begs to be read out loud because it is short, snappy, and full of images—it has the potential to be a great piece of theatre.

"A Bad Day" written by Carolyn Graham, appears in *Jazz Chants* (Oxford University Press, 1978).

A Bad Day

I overslept and missed my train,
slipped on the sidewalk
in the pouring rain,
sprained my ankle,
skinned my knees,
broke my glasses,
lost my keys,
got stuck in the elevator,
it wouldn't go,
kicked it twice and stubbed my toe,
bought a pen that didn't write
took it back and had a fight,
went home angry,
locked the door,
crawled into bed,
couldn't take it any more.

—Carolyn Graham

Choral Reading

One song that I recommend doing as a choral reading is "I Won't Be Left Behind," written by Jennifer Albert. The rights can be obtained through the Broken English Theatre Company: www.brokenenglishtheatre.com.

One of the most effective ways to motivate students to read is through choral reading. Students work in small groups with various kinds of texts. They read aloud different sections of the text as solos, in unison, in pairs, and in other configurations portraying character and emotion. They use different inflections and tones of voice to convey meaning.

Students are improvising with the melody of words without the usual pressure of reading out loud. They often enjoy the experience, and as I have found, reluctant readers tend to forget their fear of reading as they get caught up in the production of the piece.

Choral speaking and chanting involve experimentation, interpretation, and rehearsal of a piece of text, such as a poem or riddle. The students discuss the meaning of the text and consider who might be speaking and to whom. The group experiments with the language, exploring rhythm, cadence, volume, and pace. They find the energy or pulse of the poem as they read it over and over again. What is the attitude, the emotion, and the perspective?

I ask the students to find their favorite lines and try to explain why they love those lines. How do they relate to what the poem is saying? I sometimes give different stanzas to each group.

Choral reading allows students to play with words, roles, gestures, attitudes, tempo, repetition, beat, harmony, and timing. Students embody the words and find ways of saying the lines in solo, duets, and trios, or as a large group. They learn about language as they negotiate together to come up with a way to present the poem with energy, commitment, and joy. Compared with the more stylized Readers Theatre, choral reading and Story Theatre (described later in this chapter) are much more energetic, relying on more than voice to bring the text to life for an audience. The following poem, written by a Grade 7 student, works well as a choral reading.

I Ain't Moving: Poem for Rosa Parks

Get on the bus
No smile, just a frown
I'm tired, I'm hot
And I can't sit down
Well, I guess I could sit down
If I wanted to sit in the back
Plenty of seats in the front
I don't understand that!

I paid my fare
Full fare in fact
But I can't sit in the front
Only the back
"Rome wasn't built in a day," my momma once said
"You must follow your heart,
and fight with your head."
We're in a battle that we will continue to lose
unless someone stands up,
or someone don't move!

Well it's another day and here comes the bus
I've made up my mind
I'm gonna do this for us!
I get on the bus and go straight for the seat
sit down; dress spread out real neat
look around, ALL EYES ON ME!
"Get up gal!"
I heard the white man yell
I wanted to tell him to go straight to hell
but instead I said (with my voice real soothing)
"No sir, I'm tired and I ain't moving."

Well, I didn't move
I kid you not
and the more I sat
the madder he got
I still didn't move and the yelling didn't stop
and when I did I had help from the cops
Yeah, they took me to jail
but that was just fine
I had used my head and followed my mind.

Well, 45 years later
it's a brand new day
you can sit in the front seat every day.

Listen to me children
listen to me well
to the words I say, not just the story I tell.
Believe in yourself
to your beliefs be true.
Don't let nobody walk over you.
Some battles are winning ones
while others may be losing,
but stand your ground, keep your faith
and tell them
YOU AIN'T MOVIN!

—Fianah

Readers Theatre

It may be that as a culture we are losing our ear because we have consigned good English to the printed page; because we define literature as what is written to be read silently; because we are not judging language with our ears as well as our intelligence. In the torrents of words that drown our culture, have we forgotten how to listen?
—Robert MacNeil

Readers Theatre is a sophisticated form of choral reading. Students read material in small groups conveying meaning of material that is not normally meant for performance. The group members decide on focus, timing, pacing, roles, voice intonation, and pauses. They try the material many different ways before they set it for performance. I encourage the students to "see" the action in their heads and project that vision to the audience. They do not have to memorize the script, but they need to know it well if they are going to read it fluently and effectively to the rest of the class or an outside group.

In traditional Readers Theatre, students dress completely in black and sit on stools. Music stands hold their texts in place for them to read. When students present, they sit on the chairs or stools and look above the heads of their audience at a designated spot on the back wall. As the members of the audience watch and listen, they imagine the scene that the actors are "playing."

Movement is minimal. When I work with students, however, they often find that a particularly significant movement by one character, several characters, or the whole group greatly enhances the dramatic impact of one line or word. They might want to turn their backs at the end, gesture at a certain point, or have one person sit down at a significant moment to make the piece dramatically compelling.

In Readers Theatre, the narrator's voice must be heard so it is best to have students discuss how they are going to deal with the "he said" and "she exclaimed" parts of the material. In rehearsal, I encourage them to seamlessly read these words without changing tone or inflection, and students are usually amazed at how well that works.

Readers Theatre can draw on students with different levels of English proficiency. I used an excerpt from *Charlie Wilcox's Great War* by Sharon E. McKay (pages 50–53) with a Grade 9 class. There were about 16 ELL students in a class of 32 so I divided the ELL students evenly around in the four groups. The ELL students were at various levels of English language proficiency. The ones at the lowest level were asked to provide the sound effects of the battle. The ELL students had to follow along and insert appropriate noises in the script. The lines were punctuated with sounds of war and the theatrical effect was brilliant.

Student Performance Checklist

- ❑ Do we know what we want to say?

- ❑ Have we tried different ways to say it?

- ❑ Have we made sure that we tried everyone's ideas?

- ❑ Are important moments rehearsed well enough so that the audience will understand?

- ❑ Have we built the performance to some sort of climax?

- ❑ Have we layered our work so that it has some kind of form?

- ❑ Have we juxtaposed scenes or lines so that they come together in an effective way?

- ❑ Does the piece have a strong beginning? a strong ending?

- ❑ Have we incorporated effective, rehearsed transitions?

- ❑ Have we tried to incorporate some stillness and pausing in the piece for effect?

- ❑ Is everyone involved?

- ❑ Can everyone be seen?

- ❑ Does everyone look strong?

- ❑ Can everyone be heard? If not, should we find a way of combining our voices so that they are?

- ❑ Could we use the performance space in a more imaginative way?

- ❑ What more do we need to cut or change to make the piece work?

The students used their voices in different ways to re-enact the scene. Urgent, emotional dialogue contrasted with the more detached multi-voiced narrator. The background cacophony of war sounds was used sparingly at strategic points, making the reading dramatic and heart wrenching. The class felt empowered by their stirring presentation.

A group of Grade 12 students who were doing a research project on Margaret Atwood worked with this excerpt of *Oryx and Crake*. The tone of the reading was detached and cold. The lines were divided up brilliantly—the students spent lots of time working with the text—and they used all the techniques they had been taught. At the end of their presentation, other students wanted to read the book—they had been so entranced by the effect of this short passage.

"What is toast?" says Snowman to himself, once they've run off.

Toast is when you take a piece of bread—What is bread? Bread is when you take some flour—What is flour? We'll skip that part, it's too complicated. Bread is something you can eat, made from a ground-up plant and shaped like a stone You cook It ... Please why do you cook it? Why don't you just eat the plant? Never mind that part—Pay attention. You cook it and then you cut it into slices, and you put a slice into a toaster, which is a metal box that heats up with electricity—What is electricity? Don't worry about that.

While the slice is in the toaster, you get the butter—butter is a yellow grease, made from the mammary glands of—skip the butter. So, the toaster turns the slice of bread black on both sides with smoke coming out, and then this "toaster" shoots the slice up into the air and it falls onto the floor...

"Forget it," says Snowman. "Let's try again." Toast was a pointless invention from the Dark Ages. Toast was an implement of torture that caused all those subjected to it to regurgitate in verbal form the sins and crimes of their past lives. Toast was a ritual item devoured by fetishists in the belief that it would enhance their kinetic and sexual powers. Toast cannot be explained by any rational means.

Toast is me.

I am toast.

From *Oryx and Crake* by Margaret Atwood © 2003. Published by McClelland & Stewart Ltd. Used with permission of the publisher.

Story Theatre

Story Theatre is a technique for dramatizing narratives. As the text of the story is read aloud or delivered from memory by actors representing the narrator and the characters, the action is captured in movement, voice, sound effects, and possibly music. The actors fill out the narration with their own actions. Sometimes, a character takes up the narration speaking as a storyteller rather than as a character.

The material that best lends itself to Story Theatre is simple narrative: stories from the oral tradition, such as myths, fables, legends, folktales, or other powerful stories that call for action and dialogue. Elementary students especially enjoy

Suggestive Costumes

hats
scarves
gloves
shawls
jackets
uniforms
aprons

Props

books
dolls
old photographs
canes
jewellery
purses
suitcases
tickets
keys
flowers
medals
letters
paintbrushes/palettes

performing and watching Story Theatre. It is an ideal technique for secondary school students to use in performing for younger ones.

The goal of Story Theatre is to suggest rather than explicate, to enhance the imaginative and poetic qualities of a tale, symbolizing its drama rather than stating or elaborating it. Actors work with only the simplest, most suggestive props, if any, and use suggestive costumes at most. Ordinary objects may symbolize elements in the setting and can sometimes be used to represent more than one object. For instance, a ladder can be a set of steps, a window, a balcony, a mountain, or heaven—all at different points in the story.

Deciding how to divide up the text is part of the creative process of Story Theatre. Here are some of the options to consider:

- One person narrates throughout.
- Each actor does the appropriate narration as well as the character's lines—everything is memorized.
- The group plays the narrator as a chorus while the actors interpret character through words and actions.
- One group is the narrator, one group reads the dialogue, and one group does the actions. This arrangement works well with the whole class or with groups of six members.

Readers should experiment with who is to say what lines when. They can play many roles and dialogue can be improvised if that will contribute to the effectiveness of the piece. A summary of Story Theatre features appears as an appendix.

Drama Anthologies

If students are studying a topic that interests them, they can present their insights in a short anthology presentation. They need to research source material that connects to the theme and then bring this material to life through voice and movement. Students might want to create an anthology on topics such as Stop Drunk Driving, Healthy Relationships, and Drug Awareness. They have to find sources to dramatize. Statistics can be chorally read with real impact; poignant scenes can emerge from personal testimonials; movement pieces can be created from magazine and Internet pictures; and scenes can be prepared from newspaper stories and police reports.

A reproducible page outlines aspects of drama anthologies for students.

Introducing Drama Anthologies

As a group, decide on a topic or theme that interests you. Your goal is to take that topic or theme and build a dramatic presentation that draws on your personal knowledge plus the information you have gleaned from your research.

Your initial task is to illustrate this topic using three poems, three pieces of prose, and the words and/or music of one song.

You will be required to stage the material in the most *dramatically effective* way possible.

The material should be put together in such a way that the message to the audience is clear and the theatre experience unique.

Material for your anthology project can come from newspapers, stories, novels, the Internet, play scripts, poetry, music, pictures, and media.

Your group must use five of the following presentational options in the staging of the anthology:

tableaux	Readers Theatre
machines	Story Theatre
chants	soundscapes
movement	improvisational sketches
choral reading	mirrors
collage of personalities	

Plan to write your script by improvising from the source. Get up on your feet as soon as you have collected the required number of sources. Experiment with all the ideas presented. Don't reject somebody's idea until you have done some work on it.

Focus on smooth transitions between each scene, and pay special attention to the beginning and ending of your anthology.

The end result of all your labor will be a well-rehearsed, structurally unified dramatic presentation of 10 minutes duration.

Deadlines:

All sources due: _____

Preliminary script due***: _____

Presentation dates: _____

***The script, of course, will need revisions and additions, but the list of sources being used, the core ideas, the dialogue, and the movement should be recorded and written out in good form by that date.

Criteria for Presenting Material

Some ways of exploring text, such as choral reading and jazz chants, can, of course, be treated as performances for the whole class, for other classes, for assemblies, and for special evenings; however, the presentation ideas that follow are associated especially with performance for an audience. First, though, are some general principles about presenting material.

Just as we would not ask students to write a formal essay without giving them lots of ideas, practice, hints, templates, and time to develop their skills, we should be careful about asking students to speak publicly before they can do so with confidence, skill, and awareness of what makes an oral presentation work. For many adults, speaking in public is extraordinarily difficult—chanting and choral reading can help students find their public voices in ways that allow them to speak out loud with others. Because they are presenting their work in groups and reading with others in unison, students are not as exposed as they would be if reading solo to a group.

We need to carefully set up safe contexts for oral work so that students gradually become used to this kind of presentation and get better and better at it as they are given different kinds of oral tasks. Dorothy Heathcote reminds us not to place students in situations where they will be "stared" at.

I like to begin simply and then move on to more difficult tasks. Students work in partners at first, reading a selection out loud or improvising in an interview situation; then, in small groups, they find a way to divide up the text so that everyone has a chance to read or they adopt roles and improvise a scene, such as a family argument. There is no audience but themselves and they are trying on roles, working through everyone's ideas. They can then work in a large-group setting, such as a whole-class role-play with the teacher in role. Only when they are ready do they speak solo to the whole class. Speaking in public requires skill, modelling, and awareness, but the most important part of the undertaking is to give students a reason to speak, to allow them to express something that is important to them.

When students rehearse in groups, I give them some guidelines to help the process along. I ask them to

- experiment and play with the material as long as they can without setting it;
- make sure that they listen to everyone's suggestions;
- get up on their feet early and try out different ideas;
- layer voices, use repetition, and find a way of producing a collage of scenes that give different perspectives on the topic;
- find a strong beginning to their piece; and
- establish an effective, memorable ending.

In my workshop "Making Drama Presentable," I outline these principles for my student teachers:

- The presented material needs to be worthwhile, to be about something that is important in students' lives and that they want to say something about. They might want to do a presentation against smoking or on students' rights and responsibilities. They need to feel committed to the project.
- The students need to be interested in the topic and want to do the work.

- The students should be exposed to a number of drama forms and groupings—solos, duos, small group, and whole class—so that they will be able to experiment and finally choose the techniques that will best cast meaning on what they want to say.
- Adequate time and space must be devoted to the project.
- There needs to be someone outside the group, likely the teacher, who can give direction and advice.

Ask your students to check in with you once they have the answers to the questions on "Student Performance Checklist" and have worked with the material so that it can be presented for feedback from a supportive group of peers.

Reading aloud to an audience can be intimidating if one is alone. However, the activities in this chapter allow students to work collectively in small groups with texts that lend themselves to performance. Students find themselves negotiating for meaning as they analyze the structure of a text, identify with the characters' personalities and motives, create the setting through sound and movement, find props and costumes that symbolize important themes in the script, and use their voices in various ways to make an impact on their audience. I love watching ELL students be captivated by English—the new language that they are learning—as they are supported by their peers doing these kinds of activities. They seamlessly blend into the performances and take risks that they would never take on their own. Reading out loud becomes a pleasurable experience for all students as they find ways to stage the pages taken from Shakespeare to Atwood or from Greek myths to modern raps.

6. Mine for Meaning

One story I love to tell concerns one of my best friends—a teacher—and what happened when her daughter was in Kindergarten. My friend attended the parent–teacher night. The Kindergarten teacher said many kind and positive things about Emily, but at the end of the interview she said she had one concern. It was the fact that Emily, in her painting and drawing, tended to "rush her trees."

That story reminds me how teachers and students are often the victims of the rush towards knowledge. The curriculum that most teachers work with is crowded. There seems to be so much material to cover. There is little time to spend with students to allow them to play with language, tinker with text, and "mine" stories, images, poetry, and illustrations for meaning. Yet all these things are necessary if students are to develop critical literacy: to attain a deep understanding of what is read, to know where and when to apply new information, to use language appropriately in varied contexts, and more. The literacy demands placed on our students are immediate, varied, and sometimes quite complex. Students are expected to be able to read and write texts, such as reports, textbooks, online advertisements, proposals, e-mails, blogs, text messages, and texts embedded in other texts, such as on Web sites. They need to be able to evaluate what they are reading and to discriminate between what might be truth and might not.

I am aware that I am a teacher who tends to "rush her trees." I am learning, as I work with pre-service candidates and as a guest in classrooms with students I get to know only superficially, to slow down my teaching and allow more time for the group work that I so diligently set up. I want my student teachers to understand that it sometimes takes time for all of the students to understand what is being taught and that helping students with certain aspects of language learning, such as how to create and use metaphors, is worth the time it takes.

Make a Metaphor

The greatest thing by far is to have a command of metaphor.
—Aristotle, *The Poetics*

I was asked to work with a Grade 8 class to help them identify and then create their own metaphors. After I accepted the invitation, I decided to take a different approach than my usual one. I wanted students to understand that metaphors illustrate something important through comparison, but also that the juxtaposition of words and images gives them their "punch." I wanted them to see that metaphors enable people to understand one thing by seeing it in terms of another. I wanted them to use metaphors in their writing.

I decided to give them a list of metaphors that we use every day, a list of famous metaphors, and some from the novel that they were reading (*Island of the Blue Dolphins*). Once they were hooked on metaphor, they might then feel confident enough to analyze them and write some of their own.

We began by generating lists of metaphors that occur in everyday life.

Put-downs

He is not the sharpest knife in the drawer.

I don't think that she is playing with a full deck.

You *always* forget. You are such an airhead.

Compliments

You are the cream in my coffee.

My new baby girl is the apple of my eye.

Your essay has a lot of meat and potatoes. Now it's time to work towards a mouth-watering dessert.

The gruff mechanic was a diamond in the rough.

He was very top drawer.

Emotional metaphors

I blew my stack and yelled at them all.

Finally, my father dropped the bomb and told us he was leaving for good.

I'm banging my head against a brick wall.

Family metaphors

I'm the ham in the sandwich.

I was born the rose between two thorns.

My grandmother was always at the helm of the ship.

Metaphors of understanding

The seed was planted in my mind. I began to water it and let the sun shine down on the idea for a few days. Soon I knew exactly what to do.

The layers of the onion began to be peeled off and I saw my so-called friends for what they truly were.

My journey to know myself has been difficult. There have been many rockslides and storms along the way. At last, the clouds are lifting and I know I will achieve my goals.

Then, we began to write our own. I followed the steps below to provide an example and then students made their own metaphors.

1. Choose a noun.
2. Ask yourself, "What thing can I compare it to?" Choose another noun.
3. Make your comparison without using a word of comparison such as *like* or *as* and by choosing a verb in between. Example: Taking the noun *umbrella* and comparing it to a roof—The umbrella was a roof over my head.

Student Samples

The hot seat evolved into an electric chair of dissent.
Snow is a blanket of forgiveness.
The river was a ribbon of friendship.
The argument turned into a tantrum of lies.
My conversation with the guidance counsellor finally gave me a stairway to success.

Then we played Metaphor Bingo! If you would like to do this, have the students work in partners and hand out the worksheet provided. The students' goal is to create six metaphorical sentences using the words and phrases only once on the sheet. Once the students have come up with their six sentences, have them read them aloud to the class. Can the class improve on the metaphors? Can they extend them?

Here are two samples based on the worksheet: The **photograph of the lost child** kept the **invisible doors** of hope alive in her **heart**. His **journey** to freedom was a **rocky path** filled with **harsh winds** and **silent sorrow**.

Metaphor Bingo!

In partners, work to create up to six metaphorical sentences without using any words or phrases on this worksheet more than once.

Possessions	Earthly Elements	Human Feelings	Human Actions
invisible doors	rocky path	anger	drawing a first breath
mirrors	ancient gardens	dread	saying words of farewell
photograph of the lost child	harsh winds	sympathy	keeping secrets
heart	the rose	silent sorrow	war
doorways	the moon	Tear-stained face	journey
the open suitcase	constant thunder	guilt	locking up
flags	smoke	jealousy	hiding
veil	earth	love	marching
abandoned cars	snowflakes	happiness	departing

Create Minimal Scripts

In one of my most successful writing exercises, young adolescents create and read their own scripts by cutting and pasting dialogue from magazines and newspapers. Working with partners, they scan magazines for interesting phrases, sentences, and words that pack some kind of punch. They cut them out and lay them all out on a colored sheet of paper. Their clippings will evolve into scripts of about eight lines.

They then begin to "play" with the language. Some students decide right away what the play could be about. Others are confident enough to let the script have many meanings and they explore the script, changing the *who, where,* and *what is happening.* Only when they are confident with the meaning that they have created should they "glue" the words to the paper.

Students then rehearse the script by reading it out loud. I encourage them to read the script with different kinds of emotions and in different contexts. I get them to look at the color that the text is in or the size of the words, and to read the lines based on how the words look.

Next, each pair passes the script on to another pair. The second pair creates meaning out of the words that have been created by others. Partners are not allowed to talk to the original writers/creators. They are not allowed to change the words or the order of the words, but they can certainly change the punctuation to create a different meaning.

For instance, one pair of students that I worked with created the first lines of their script this way.

Man: The police say that there are no suspects at this time.
Woman: For sure?
Man: Whatever you thought, think again.

Their partner group changed the meaning of the original script entirely by having the characters put the lines together in different ways.

Reporter: The police say that there are no suspects at this time. For sure.
Boss: Whatever.
Reporter: You thought….
Boss: Think again.

We then share the texts with the rest of the class, juxtaposing the same script with different actors and different interpretations.

One fascinating thing about this exercise is that students become critically aware of what works theatrically and what does not. They begin to see how crucial punctuation is to writing and how little dashes on the page can make a world of difference.

I have used *Eats, Shoots & Leaves* with classes as I work in this way. The students begin to understand what Lynne Truss means when she tells us that "punctuation is a courtesy designed to help readers to understand a story without stumbling." They love the example she uses:

A woman, without her man, is nothing.

A woman: without her, man is nothing. (p. 9)

What's It All About?

The resource "Overheard Conversations" provides short conversations between two people. You might ask students to interpret these as if they are overhearing them or to create similar minimal scripts. In partners, they can create the place and the circumstances that have brought these people together saying these lines. All they need is imagination!

Students choose the minimal script that they want to work with. In their pairs, they decide who is going to read each role. After they have read the script through out loud once, they discuss with their partners who they think these characters might be, where they might be saying these lines to one another, and why they are having this conversation. Encourage students to try many different characters, locations, and situations.

After a while, have students switch roles and continue trying to find the most authentic way to read their script. Tell them that when they feel they have got the meaning just right, they should read the script out loud to another partner group. That group should offer suggestions for making it better. Are longer pauses needed between lines? Would props make the scene more believable? Does a role need to be taken more seriously? Should either actor speak more loudly to be better heard?

Eventually, the pairs present their minimal scripts to the class and students guess who they are, where they are, and what is happening.

Tinker with Text

I love revisions. Where else in life can spilled milk be transformed into ice cream?
—Katherine Paterson

Artists who became great masters first copied great paintings, and as they worked with the same lines, colors, designs, and relationships, they began to find their own style.

I recommend taking a somewhat similar approach to writing, using accessible pieces of literature—excerpts from novels, poems or parts of poems, historical accounts, scripts of graphic novels, and the whole array of writing that is found in newspapers (e.g., obituaries, editorials, personal columns, letters to the editor, and advertisements). Students can use these source materials to tinker with text, play with language, meddle with juxtaposition, vocabulary, voice, and layout so that they become comfortable working with text, finding words and patterns of language that they love, seeing how the authors use language to entertain, question, predict, grieve, gripe, admit, and long for. I find that adolescents sometimes need to tinker with the language of others in a hands-on way so that they begin to feel more comfortable thinking about and editing their own creations.

It is important to model how to "tinker." You could conduct a guided writing class so that students see you as someone who is willing to throw things out, start again, ask for help, leave the writing alone, and come back to it with a clearer mind. Inviting a professional writer into the class to talk about revising is also a good idea. On page 63, you will find two tinkering activities involving newspapers in the classroom.

Overheard Conversations

What you are about to read are "minimal scripts," or short conversations between two people. You and a partner are going to create the place and the circumstances that have brought these people together saying these lines. All you need is your imagination!

Do you have to go there again?
Yes.
Well, fine, then.

Why did you have to say that?
What?
It's always this way.

I swear that I didn't mean to do it.
Yeah?
I swear.

I have been meaning to ask you something.
What?
Oh, never mind.

Are you going to tell her?
I don't know. Do you think I should?
It's not for me to say.

I don't know why it always has to end up this way.
What does?
This.

Tell me everything is going to be all right.
I can't do that.
Why not?

Who is this?
Really?
Wow. I would never have thought.

Don't touch that.
But it's mine.
Who says?

I'm ready now.
Forget it.

But you promised.
I know I did. It's just …
It's just what?
It doesn't matter.

Take a chance.
Why should I?
Why not?

Becoming News Story Editors: One way to get students to look at juxtaposition is to cut five stories out of the newspaper. In groups of five or six, the students read the stories and then arrange them in order of importance. They need to think about their audience and what will sell the newspaper. Which will be the lead story? What headline will they give it? What is the least important story? Once they have completed the layout of the newspaper, prompt them to compare their layouts with those of another group. Each group must be able to defend its design. You might have the students compare their decisions with the real newspaper edition.

Analyzing Newspaper Language: Divide the class into groups. Give each group a page from a different section of the newspaper: front page; feature page, such as the travel section; editorial page; obituaries; comics; sports; business. Ask each group to choose one paragraph from their page and to copy this paragraph out onto a sheet of paper. Then have them analyze the kind of writing by answering the following questions.

- Is there a straightforward delivery of facts?
- Are the sentences long or short?
- Are the words neutral or loaded with emotion?
- Is there evidence of a personal voice?
- Is the writer opinionated or neutral?
- Are the thoughts complicated or simple?
- Does the style make the text easy to read?
- Are the sentences expected to make people think logically or react emotionally?
- Is the language colorful and vivid? Or, is it plain and dull?

Then, have the students in their groups alter the language entirely so that the meaning and effect of the story or text is changed.

Graphic Novel Exercises

Graphic novels are becoming very popular texts to read, and their availability has meant that in many school libraries, the circulation has increased enormously. Teachers can motivate readers, especially reluctant readers or readers at risk, to become successfully engaged with this accessible and entertaining form of narrative.

Here are two activities that harness the literacy power of the graphic novel.

I See, I Wonder, I Remember, I Imagine …: Due to their visual nature, graphic novels provide a visceral, immediate experience. Students gravitate to them because of the variety of images, colors, situations, and relationships that are on the cover or "Splash page," where the title, illustrations, and credits appear. Before you introduce a class of students to graphic novels, encourage them to spend time looking at photographs or drawings on an overhead. I use a standard template for this activity.

I see … I wonder … I remember … I imagine …

We discuss what the students see. I am able to gauge their visual literacy, which is usually surprisingly sophisticated. I then show them the cover or Splash page of a graphic novel and prompt them to predict what it is about. They record their first impressions of the images and words on the Splash page in a similar kind of template and then they talk about these thoughts with a partner or in small groups.

Framing the Experience: In groups of four, students focus on a page in a graphic novel that they are reading. The page needs the following features: at least three characters, captions, sound effects, speech bubbles, and thought bubbles. Ask students to work on creating the panels: bringing to life the language in the speech and thought bubbles, creating the movement from panel to panel, and devising the sound effects. Encourage them to represent as precisely as possible the images and words portrayed in this section of the novel. A narrator could read the captions, other students could add sound effects, and other students could read the language in the speech and thought bubbles. Let the students experiment with different kinds of voices and movements. When one frame ends, make use of a signal, such as a drumbeat, to indicate that the story has moved to the next panel. Each group could share its work with another group in the class.

Taking time out to hone skills and play with words, symbols, and metaphor is essential if we are to help students use language in a variety of situations for a number of different reasons. I want students to have the power of words at their fingertips and to use language in interesting ways to make sense of the world in which they live.

I remember the moment I understood that my daughter was well on her road to literacy. We were driving to our country home after a difficult day in school and piles of homework awaited her that evening. Our long concession road is muddy and rutted at the best of times, and on this rainy, wet, windy day, we came over the crest of the hill to see a sign, "ROUGH ROAD AHEAD." Jessica turned to me and asked, "Do you suppose that is a metaphor?" We laughed despite ourselves. I knew then that language could be a source of comfort and joy to her as well as a means of thinking about things on many levels and of helping her live well in the world. That is what we hope for our students.

7. Inside Images

Cameras don't take great pictures. Artists take great pictures. And no two artists see the same things the same way.

—Nan Goldin

Elliot Eisner reminds us that "the arts make vivid the fact that neither words in their literal form nor numbers exhaust what we can know. The limits of our language do not define the limits of our cognition." I know that many students can communicate what they understand through their bodies in movement or through a tableau, drawing, or sculpture. Students can communicate very complex feelings and ideas through the arts. Literacy goes beyond the written word.

Students live in a visual world. They are saturated with images on the computer, on the Internet, on TV, and in films as well as sophisticated advertising. These images are powerful and can affect students in many different ways.

As teachers, we need to help students recognize how images are being used to influence them in all of the contexts where they meet them. Students need to be aware of how images are juxtaposed so that they can begin to "see" their historical and cultural significance and thereby deconstruct how the messages are being conveyed. Once students can interpret visual messages, they have control over the information and can be critically, visually literate.

Start with Art—Deconstructing Magazine Ads

One of the best ways to start with art is to have students look hard and deeply at pictures of advertisements in magazines. Advertisers design ads very carefully by composing the elements in a picture to generate certain effects. Often, they overlay words to work with the image to influence the reader.

"Taking a Critical Look at Pictures and Texts" raises some questions I use when I work with students. (See page 66.) You might want to adopt the questions for your students.

Taking a Critical Look at Pictures and Texts

When looking at a media advertisement, be sure to consider these questions:

- What are all of the objects or props that are included in the picture? How are they used?

- What kinds of actors are chosen to represent the product? Who "speaks" and who is silent? What kind of body language is being used? How do the facial expressions influence the viewer?

- Take a look at the camera angles. Are there close-ups? long shots? medium-distance shots? What details are included? What is left out? What has been foregrounded and why? What is in the background? If the photographer has taken a picture from above the subject, how might that influence our feelings about the subject? How might we be influenced by the positioning of objects and people?

- Lighting is a photographer's most powerful resource. Putting the subject in front of the light source can produce a silhouette, highlighting shapes rather than detail. What is lit? What is in shadow? What does that say? How do the text and images come together to give a message?

- Sometimes, photographers blur details and outlines in a photo. How does the photographer use sharp and soft focus? What effect might that have on us?

- Look at the text. How many words? How are the words positioned in the ad? Are they in **bold** type, *italicized* type, or small case?

- What other kinds of technology and artistic devices were used in the ad to influence the reader? How effective are they?

- Why were all of these decisions made? What is overtly stated? What is inferred? Do you feel manipulated? Do you think others would feel manipulated?

Close Relations: Life and Art

As part of an ArtsApproach project in the Art Gallery at York University, I worked with a senior-level photography class who were visiting the work of contemporary artist Jeremy Deller. Drawing inspiration from Deller's commitment to document and celebrate unrecorded or overlooked histories, Allyson Adley, the education director, and I wanted to help students research and represent their own communities' hidden histories.

After their initial viewing of the Deller exhibition, I asked students to write down some of their own personal histories. For instance, I asked them to consider what they have in the foreground in their lives and what they wished could stay in the background. What voices were absent from their lives? Who or what in their lives was overlooked in some way? I asked them to get into partners and discuss some of these ideas.

I then asked them to take their partners with them and stand by the piece of Deller's work to which they could best relate in some way. They told their partners what they were thinking. Only after they had worked their ideas in discussion with their partners did I ask them to tell the class about them. One boy stood beside a painting depicting a man with needles coming out of his ears and a figure walking away. He told the class that he related to the figure walking away from the drug addict, who was his father. Other stories were as riveting. Challenging contemporary art was unlocking personal stories that would then be documented in photography and text by the students

Later, students took photographs of their selected subjects. For instance, one student took pictures of her grandfather's solitary existence in her family's house; she juxtaposed these images with those taken in the busy variety store next door to the house. All of the students kept journals of their research, recording conversations with family and community members, which provided the basis of their final texts. These were then displayed alongside the photographs in an exhibition on the York University campus.

After the development of the pictures, the students took part in a curatorial session in which they selected the photographs that appeared in the exhibition. Participants also learned about the installation process. Friends and family of the participants were invited to a reception in celebration of the exhibition opening.

A Figure Full of Words

Often, a graphic organizer, such as Role on the Wall, will help students generate ideas for discussion and writing.

1. Ask for a volunteer to draw on the chalkboard a large abstract figure of a character in one of the stories that the class is reading. The figure should be large enough so that students can write descriptive words and phrases inside it. The name of the character could be written within the figure.

2. On the inside of the figure, class members write as many words that describe the person's psychological, emotional, and physical characteristics as possible.

3. Now, in the space surrounding the figure, they write words that describe the difficulties that the person is encountering.

4. Around the figure, the names of people or things that are supporting this person are written. The students watch as the figure fills up with words. A good idea is to play music in the background and have two or three people at a time record their thoughts.

5. After everyone has had a chance to contribute words, conduct a whole-class discussion about the words generated. You might want students to copy the figure into their binders.

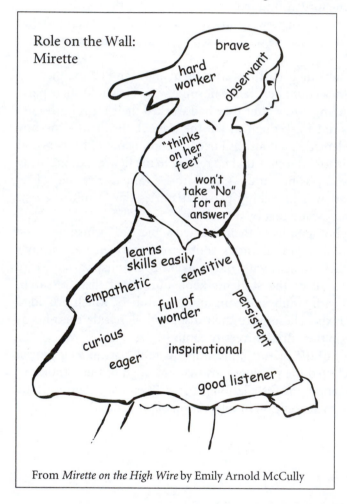

Role on the Wall: Mirette

From *Mirette on the High Wire* by Emily Arnold McCully

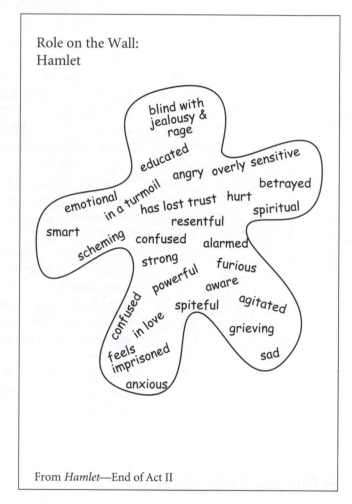

Role on the Wall: Hamlet

From *Hamlet*—End of Act II

Move into Understanding

Students have a far greater capacity than has been assumed to articulate their ideas and understandings through their bodies in dance and with imagined voices in dramatic contexts.

Why use movement in your classroom?

- It motivates students to work collaboratively in groups.
- It promotes problem solving.
- It encourages the use of the body as an expressive medium—movement is a type of literacy.
- It helps students communicate what they know and value in a way that is sometimes even more powerful than the spoken or written word.
- It can enable powerful discussion by first permitting students to embody experiences.
- It provides an opportunity for students to let their imaginations flow freely.
- It develops concentration and self-confidence.
- It provides an opportunity for physical exercise and aids in physical co-ordination.

As you begin incorporating movement into your lessons, don't worry about the skill level of your students. As students learn more about movement and develop a movement vocabulary, their bodies will become more expressive and controlled, and their movement, more abstract.

Moves for Partners

Here are some simple movement activities to begin with.

I can do this; I can do that: Students find partners and decide who is *A* and who is *B*. The *A*s begin by making a movement with one of their arms and saying, "I can do this." The *B*s mirror the movement exactly and say, "I can do that." Initially, movements will be of the occupational kind (e.g., brushing teeth). Encourage abstract movement starting with the arms only. A good idea is to have students sitting facing one another on the floor so that they can use only their upper bodies.

Stop the exercise and indicate that you want the *B*s to initiate the movement. This time the movement and the sentence "I can do this" should be very slow. The *A*s mirror the movements and slow speech.

Mirrors: After some experimenting, ask the students not to speak. The *A*s continue to follow the *B*s. Add music to the movement so that students can get caught up in the experience. "Trois Gymnopedies" by Eric Satie and Debussy's "Claire de Lune" are good choices because of their slow tempo and mood.

I rely a lot on the music of Rafael Fuentes—some of which has been composed for teachers to use in their classrooms. For more information on CDs, check out www.soundtracksound.com.

Explore How Things Work

a) **Water Purification Machines:** Junior students love making machines with their bodies. During one Earth Week, I worked with a Grade 6 class that had serious concerns about the degradation of the environment. They lived in a rural community near Lake Simcoe, Ontario, and were outraged that on many summer weekends their local beach was closed because the water was polluted. Their teacher had been teaching them about water purification and had taken them to a water purification plant the week before my visit. I created an exercise that the teacher thought would be a great summative assessment task. I organized the students in groups of six and asked them to demonstrate through movement what they had learned about the water purification process.

First, students individually sketched what they remembered about the machine at the water purification plant. They then compared their sketches with those of a partner and finally checked out the machine in the official handout which the teacher had received.

Next, I asked the students to create the whole machine in groups using people's bodies as the machine parts and appointing a spokesperson to explain how the machine worked. One group asked whether each individual part could have a "voice" and I agreed—I realized that if I incorporated that suggestion, I would have a strong performance task where individuals could demonstrate their understandings, synthesize their experiences, and propose alternatives.

b) Wonder Machines: I worked with a group of Grades 6, 7, and 8 Special Education students who were learning about environmental issues. In groups, they brainstormed all the problems of the world and then listed the top five problems facing the planet.

By consensus, each group chose one problem that members, as scientists, wanted to rectify: they were to create a machine that would solve the problem. They used voice and movement; and a spokesperson explained the machine to the rest of the class at a Top Scientists Convention featuring Wonder Machines to save the planet. Each group produced a technical booklet that explained how the machine worked.

If you would like to do this activity with your students, refer to the reproducible page "Wonder Machines" in the Appendixes.

The teacher was amazed that the students took the task seriously and thrilled by the technical booklets and sketches that they prepared as a summative task. The booklets were on display on parents' night and many parents talked about how their children had loved the experience.

Embody the Dynamics of Power

I was asked to work with a group of Grade 10 students who were interested in and willing to look at the topics of racism and bullying. I wanted to begin the series of workshops with exploring the dynamics of power through movement:

1. I divided the class into groups of three and directed the students to name themselves A, B, or C.
2. I asked the As "to create a frozen statue that represented some kind of power and prestige." I gave them some examples—a royal figure, a boss, a chief of some kind.
3. I asked the Bs to stand by the As in neutral positions.
4. Then I asked the Cs to fit themselves into the pictures that had been created by the As and Bs, but to assume frozen stances of oppression in relation to the images of power already created.
5. Next, I played music from *Meet Joe Black* and directed the As to walk across the room, find a spot, and reverse their stance so that they now created rep-

resentations of oppressed persons. Once the *A*s were in frozen positions, the *B*s were directed to move across the room and create neutral positions in relation to the *A*s.

6. I then asked the *C*s to cross the room and insert themselves into the pictures by creating positions of power over the other individuals.

7. The groups continued to do their high, medium, and low status switches to the music.

The discussion that followed centred on the feelings of the *B*s who had to remain in a neutral position. Their comments were interesting. They said that they felt uncomfortable because they were drawn to be part of the dominator's world, but sympathized with the oppressed.

We continued with work on Dionne Brand's brilliant poem "Blues Spiritual of Mammy Prater" (see Chapter 9 for more on this poem). After reading the poem chorally, the students explored through movement only what Mammy Prater's life might have been like. One group created a powerful scene depicting slaves working under the oppressive stance of an overseer. They had to gain his approval before they could quit work. At the overseer's side was his slave assistant who looked uncomfortable and powerless every time a slave approached the overseer. The students had incorporated the ideas of the movement exercise into their final piece.

From there, we discussed the complex life of the onlooker in oppressive situations. Our discussion took us into the range of the Holocaust, the American civil rights movement, and the internment of Japanese Canadians during the Second World War. It also encompassed students talking about their personal fears of getting involved in fights in schools and how often they turned away rather than running the risk of getting hurt. There followed a difficult, but important discussion about the role of the onlooker in bullying situations.

Make Investigations through Movement and Stillness

Through moving and making statues, students are able to investigate everything from story settings to characters to concepts to difficult knowledge about complex issues.

Investigate a Setting

Students can investigate the setting of a novel, perhaps a factory, prison camp, high-school hallway, or space station. Have them come up one by one and create the space by taking on a role. Once a student has finished moving and has frozen, another person enters the space and adds to the setting and context by creating another frozen statue. The exercise can be continued until everyone is in the space, or you can stop the activity and ask the students outside the setting what they are seeing. What are their new insights about the novel's setting?

On one memorable occasion, Grade 9 students and I worked with a graphic novel about the attack on Pearl Harbor. The students depicted in a whole-class tableau the panel of the actual attack and its effect on the American fleet. I touched on the shoulder the actors who played characters who were still alive and asked them to spontaneously create thought bubbles. Two volunteers created the sound effects of the attack.

Flocking

Flocking is a form of spontaneous movement improvisation. The group works as a collective as students shift form, sometimes following, sometimes leading one another's movement. Flocking can be explored with three or more people and used to investigate any theme, image, character, concept, or journey.

The students number themselves off in their small groups and organize themselves in a diamond formation.

Number 1 is the first leader and faces a wall or a window; the other students face the same way. When number 1 begins to move, the other students shadow or mirror the movement. After a time, number 1, as leader, rotates to the right and the other students follow the rotation so that now they are following number 2, who initiates the movement that the others shadow. Number 3 then initiates the movement; finally, number 4 does so.

The students move to music. It is best to choose slow music so that the movement can be sustained and the groups can follow one another and make easy transitions. Encourage students to experiment with different kinds of movement, changing tempo, shape, and level. If they are working with a theme, the words that they choose can relate to one another or they can be juxtaposed to create an effective jaggedness to the work.

The Wave

This movement exercise relies on a group's ability to work together and communicate non-verbally. It involves up to eight students walking, in unison, shoulder to shoulder, and spontaneously dropping out of the line to create statues or shapes that reflect the characters, themes, and emotions being explored. The exercise is beautiful to watch.

Divide the class into groups of six to eight. While one group creates the Wave, the others stand on both sides of the space to watch and reflect on the experience. Everyone gets a turn.

The working group stands at one end of the room. I encourage them to stand shoulder to shoulder in a straight line, almost touching elbows.

On my signal, the group moves forward simultaneously, crosses the room, turns around, and returns—the students maintain their close, straight formation. I encourage them to "sense each other's impulses" as they walk together.

The next step is to create statues. As the group crosses the room the second time, anyone can spontaneously "fall out" of the line and create a statue or shape that represents the character's feelings, thoughts, or reactions. The rest of the students keep walking. When the walkers turn around and come back, they envelop the statue back into the line. As they gain more confidence and skill at this exercise, students playing statues can wait for one or more Waves before being picked up—doing so allows the onlookers more time to look at their positioning. Music can be played during the exercise.

I have used the Wave to depict journeys both real and symbolic. Students have created the journey that Lucia from *The Woman Who Outshone the Sun* took after she was driven from the village. A Grade 12 English class once represented Lady Macbeth's journey into madness. The onlooker students stood at the side and watched the various statue interpretations of Lady Macbeth. I then asked the onlookers to represent the horrified, suspicious courtiers in tableau formations on either side of the classroom. One student represented Macbeth himself as a terrified onlooker within the tableaux.

Life Cycle

Have students put together a sequence of movements with tableaux (see below) symbolizing the stages of the life cycle. Using Shakespeare's imagery, have them move from birth through childhood, adolescence, adulthood, and old age to death, depicting moments that crystallize the essence of the various life stages.

> *Jaques:* All the world's a stage,
> And all the men and women merely players;
> They have their exits and their entrances,
> And one man in his time plays many parts,
> His acts being seven ages. At first, the infant,
> Mewling and puking in the nurse's arms.
> Then the whining schoolboy, with his satchel
> And shining morning face, creeping like snail
> Unwillingly to school. And then the lover,
> Sighing like furnace, with a woeful ballad
> Made to his mistress' eyebrow. Then a soldier,
> Full of strange oaths and bearded like the pard,
> Jealous in honor, sudden and quick in quarrel,
> Seeking the bubble reputation
> Even in the cannon's mouth. And then the justice,
> In fair round belly with good capon lin'd,
> With eyes severe and beard of formal cut,
> Full of wise saws and modern instances
> And so he plays his part. The sixth age shifts
> Into the lean and slipper'd pantaloon
> With spectacles on nose and pouch on side;
> His youthful hose, well sav'd, a world too wide
> For his shrunk shank, and his big manly voice,
> Turning again toward childish treble, pipes
> And whistles in his sound. Last scene of all,
> That ends this strange eventful history,
> Is second childishness and mere oblivion,
> Sans teeth, sans eyes, sans taste, sans everything.

—*As You Like It*, Act II, Scene vii

Have each group put their choreography to music that they think is appropriate and share their sequence with another class. (This exercise would be especially great to do before students see a production of *As You Like It*.)

Tableaux, or frozen images, are an excellent way of framing moments of significance that students are encountering in their reading, writing, and discussions. These frozen pictures "bottle time" and allow students to demonstrate through their bodies (using facial expressions, gesture, relationships, and levels) their understanding about what is being taught. Teachers can control the classroom environment easily and students appreciate seeing the text as well as reading it.

You might want to teach the elements of tableaux before the literacy lesson so that students know what is expected of them. Explain to students that tableaux are still images or "freeze frames" of people who represent not just a moment in time, but a *problem* in time. Encourage them to create images with their bodies that tell some kind of story: They can crystallize a key moment, idea, reaction, statement, or theme that the rest of the class as the audience can study, analyze, and discuss.

Tableaux require that students work in groups to discuss, collaborate, and select the image that they want to represent and communicate. Students might get into groups of three to create tableaux such as Baby's First Step, An Unwanted Haircut, Vice-Principal's Office: Late Again?, First Day in a New School, and Freedom: The First Moment of Summer Vacation.

For the practice session, I ask one group to volunteer as demonstrators, and before working in their groups, the whole class watches and sees how effective the technique can be. I invite students to think about and experiment with

- different levels—high, medium, low—so that the image is varied in form;
- various body shapes (open, closed) and to make sure that the important elements in the tableau can be seen by the rest of the class when the tableau is shared;
- the relationship in terms of physical distance between and among characters in the tableau;
- what the audience will focus on when the image is frozen and analyzed; and
- different kinds of emotions, body language, and facial expressions that will communicate the meaning effectively.

Tableaux before, during, and after Reading

Often, I use tableaux before reading so that I can tap into the collective prior knowledge of the students. I use them during reading to help students physically "frame" passing moments in the text, and I use them after reading so that I can assess students' collective understanding of the meaning "behind the words."

Introduce New Material

One way to elicit initial discussions when introducing new material is through tableaux crossovers. Ask the students to find partners. Have them decide who is

A and who is *B*. The *As* are to go to one side of the classroom; the *Bs* are to go to the other.

The *As* are to work together quickly to make a tableau that symbolizes war. The *Bs* are to construct a tableau that represents the opposite: peace.

With music playing, have the students trade places, experience the opposite tableau, and then transition back again. Doing such a tableau crossover is a powerful way to mark an occasion such as Remembrance Day. Students can bring in props or costumes to make the tableaux more authentic.

Let Time Stand Still

I often use this technique when I work with novels or short stories. Instead of having the students read the texts and then answer a series of questions, I have them work together in groups to create moments when time stands still. I want them to capture moments in the text that explain

- the relationships among characters;
- the sequence of events;
- how the most powerful lines in the text would look "frozen in time";
- how the setting of the novel affects the characters; and
- how objects or props play a part in the story.

The tableaux that groups develop can be shared with the class and the onlookers can deconstruct the meanings being crystallized.

Step In, Step Out

Once students have created tableaux in groups of three, I ask them to concentrate on bringing the frozen pictures to life. As a group shares an image, members step out of the picture one by one and speak lines of dialogue or improvise what the characters might speak at that moment. They then step back into the picture and allow someone else to speak.

Often, I ask students in the audience to indicate which character they would like to speak to. The classmate approaches someone in the tableau and brings that character to life by a question. The rest of the students in the tableau remain frozen as the chosen character speaks.

Tableaux with Monologues

Once students have had a chance to become comfortable bringing the tableaux to life and speaking through improvisation, they can write down those thoughts and create monologues that are heard in sequence. Have them say their monologues during a presentation and then return to the frozen picture. Sometimes, the students decide to change the picture once each member of the group has spoken.

Tableaux from Pictures

Another way to use tableaux is to find photographs and historical pictures showing people in dramatic situations, such as being on strike, immigrating, and facing some sort of difficulty—and have students re-create the scene as exactly as possible. After they do that, have them discuss each person's possible perspective and story in the picture. They could create monologues capturing those points of view or they could bring the scene to life through improvisation and tell the story of the characters in a two-minute scene.

Quick Gesture Drawing

How Art Works

Suggest that students lightly trace on tracing paper the lines that suggest the structure of a favorite painting or drawing. When they remove the paper and study the lines that they have drawn, they should gain some insight into how the artist organized the work.

After a group has composed a tableau, have the other students do quick gesture drawings without lifting their pencils or carbon from the page. Can they find the implied movement in the image? Can they then work with what they have created to make the drawing into a composition about people and the different power relationships they have with one another?

Deconstructing tableaux allows students to enter into the interior reality of a character. It also teaches students that none of us sees the same things the same way. The ambiguity of art and our response to it frees us up to have a conversation in new ways.

The arts are a form of literacy. They give students alternative ways of expressing what they know and understand. If we limit our definition of school literacy to activities related to words on a page and a pen in the hand, then we diminish the options available to awaken in our students new, creative communicative abilities. The arts teach students to think—about images, about words, about gestures, about shapes, and about relationships.

When students are invited to reveal what they are thinking and feeling through their bodies and in words related to images and music, they suddenly have many more options, many more poetic ways, to tell us who they are and what they understand.

8. Immersed in Role

What we say and how we say it depends on the social context we find ourselves in. Different contexts require different ways of talking. The language of the dance floor is not the same as the language of the courtroom. Language and literacy are therefore embedded in an awareness of how the world works, in issues of power, cultural difference, domination, and emancipation.

Talking into Understanding

I am talking about a culture of schooling in which more importance is placed on exploration than on discovering, more value is assigned to surprise than to control, more attention is devoted to what is distinctive than to what is standard, more interest is related to what is metaphorical than to what is literal.

—Elliot Eisner

We know that expert readers search for connections between what they read and what they know. Struggling readers often need to be prompted into talking about what they know of a subject before they begin reading about it. Brainstorming sessions and discussions help students "talk themselves into understanding."

In 1989, the School Oracy Project published its first magazine. In the introduction, the authors outlined the importance of talk as a teaching/learning strategy.

School opens up yet more worlds—a mass of new knowledge and information, a wider group of adults, other children. Traditionally, perhaps still to many parents, the view of school has been of the place where the chattering had to stop. The teacher talked, passing on the knowledge and information, and the children listened, soaking it up for future use. Written work and reading were individual, quiet activities, done by the child and checked by the teacher. For some time now, some educationalists have been challenging this view. Information and knowledge, they have said, cannot just be transferred like cargo being loaded from one ship on to another.

I set up situations in classrooms where students do a lot of talking as they plan, design questions and lists, interview people, role-play, and reflect on what they are experiencing and learning in the classroom. Once they have talked with a partner or in small groups, or even to the whole class using a spokesperson from their discussion groups, they are more ready to read challenging material that might include some of that vocabulary or more confident to write a response.

When I set up role-playing situations with students who lack experience, I limit the role-playing time to maybe a minute and control the interaction. I ask students to find a partner and decide on who is playing what role. When I hit a tambourine, the student pairs begin talking; when I hit the tambourine again, students stop in time and motion and "freeze." I then interview some of the students in role to find out what has occurred in the role-playing session. Role-playing allows students to "see" what they are reading and learning, as they create scenarios, apply, and play out possibilities in imagined contexts that are safe.

The Expert Game

One good way to start role-playing in small groups is to design a role-playing situation in which an interview takes place. The Expert Game is one that works. It provides students with authentic, although imagined contexts that demand oral language and allow for social interaction that has positive results. Here is how to do it.

"Number yourselves off from 1 to 5. Number 1 is going to be an expert. In this case, number 1 is going to be an underwater diver who is an expert at finding ancient treasures. The rest of you (2, 3, 4, and 5) are the owners of the international Treasure Hunt Company. You require the expertise of an underwater diver to make a series of dangerous, but lucrative discoveries.

"I want to speak to the experts privately. In the meantime, members of each interviewing team need to decide what qualities and expertise you would like this underwater diver to have and to come up with some introductory questions. Remember to make this a formal interview and to set up the scene so that all of you will be facing the interviewee."

Tell the experts in a private conversation that they are to pretend to know as much as they can about underwater diving. Encourage them to use their imaginations and to be as serious as possible about this role. Send the experts back to their groups, and then say: "On my signal, I want you to begin the interview. Invite the candidate to sit down and then begin the questioning."

The interviews last three or four minutes and then I ask one interviewer per group to stand. I pose some questions.

- At this point in the interview, what is your overall impression of the candidate? Are you leaning towards hiring him or her? Why or why not?
- What further questions would you like to ask before you make your decision?

You can use "The Expert Game—Oral Language Interview Snapshot," to assess student use of language (see the Appendixes).

After the practice session, make sure that everyone in the group has a chance to play an expert. Other expert roles include an expert detective, an expert athletic coach, an expert concert organizer, an expert teen magazine editor, and an expert body piercer.

Once, I worked with a Grade 9 class who had been reading an article about the perils of body piercing. After they had read the article, we played the Expert Game. The student volunteers demonstrated that they had understood the article by their ability to answer the questions posed by the hiring committee of health officials. The teacher and I were able to assess the students' reading comprehension of the article by listening in to the role-playing situations.

Hot-seating: Interviewing Characters Fictional and Real

General Question Categories

Consider how these can be used strategically.

Closed questions: These solicit specific facts. What facts do you want clarified? If you are interviewing Hamlet's mother Gertrude, the questions could be about where she was at the time of her husband's death.

Open questions: These have a number of possible answers. Examples: What if? Why do you think …? Is there a possibility that …? These questions often let us in on what the character is thinking and feeling.

Pseudo questions: These expect specific answers and the questioner disregards other valid answers; rhetorical questions fall into this category.

Diagnostic questions: These ascertain what students already know or have learned.

Hot-seating is an activity where the students, performing as themselves, have the opportunity to question or interview a role player who remains in character. The individual student sits in the "hot seat" at the front of the classroom and answers questions in role. I use this teaching strategy when I work with plays, novels, and historical incidents. I often help students think about the kinds of questions that they want to ask: these determine the answers.

You can hot-seat historical characters. For example, say it is 1534 and Jacques Cartier is recruiting sailors for his ships to the New World. In role as the recruitment officer, you could interview and hire sailors to make the journey. Criteria for successful selection would include a willingness to take orders, a sense of adventure, and an ability to withstand long days and hours of cold and hunger. Before you hot-seat the applicants, have them fill out application forms to serve as the basis of your questions.

Sometimes, the teacher works in role and the students, also in role, interview to obtain information. The teacher in role is able to work inside the situation, creating a climate where the honesty of individual contributions is valued and respect is shown to everyone who contributes ideas. The teacher in role imbues the situation with seriousness of purpose and adds an element of tension to the work in role. I call this teaching for tension.

I worked with a teacher in an ELL classroom where the students were newly arrived to the country and did not have much English language skill. We decided to initiate a drama in which the teacher would introduce a woman whom she had found on her porch that morning. The woman appeared to be disoriented and refused to speak, although it was obvious she could understand. The class had to find ways of getting the woman to tell her story. They became a hospital staff and set up a reception area, a waiting room for other visitors, an interview team, and student doctors who were learning how to interview patients who had been traumatized in some way.

I played the disoriented person. The students wanted to see if I had anything in my purse that might give them clues as to who I was. I had keys, a picture of a baby, and a note in English written in difficult script and with challenging words: "If you encounter this person and she appears disoriented, keep her safe, phone this number and talk to whomever answers the phone. This person has a medical condition that makes her extremely anxious. She is not dangerous and likes tea with biscuits." It was remarkable to watch these ELL students strive to speak to get the "lady on the porch" to tell her story.

From Talk into Writing

For a lesson that I conducted with a Grade 9 class of girls, I wrote Dear Amber letters and allowed the students to talk about the conflicts revealed in each letter.

First, in partners, students shared information about whom they approached when they needed advice. I asked: "Do you have a special family member or friend whom you can trust? Do you usually follow the advice given?"

After they shared that information, I introduced the three letters. One, with an accompanying student response, appears here; all letters appear in reproducible format in the Appendixes.

Dear Amber:

I am 14 years old and my father has recently remarried. His new wife's name is Cassie and she is funny, kind, and lets me have my friends over on weekends to watch movies and hang out. She also allows me to try on her clothes and experiment with her make-up. We talk a lot and get along really well. Actually, she is more like a friend than a stepmother.

The problem is that when I go home after a weekend spent with Cassie and my dad, my mom gets all moody if I tell her anything positive. She bombards me with questions about Cassie and then gets mad if I say anything about her. It's got so that I am beginning to tell her lies about Cassie so that she won't be so jealous. I am beginning to make Cassie out to be something mean and horrible just to make my mom feel better.

The other night I was telling her a stupid lie about something that Cassie had said and my mom got really mad and overprotective and phoned Cassie up and started yelling at her over the phone. I could not get her to stop. It ended with Cassie hanging up on her. Now Cassie knows that I have been telling lies about her. She must be really hurt.

What do I say to Cassie the next time I see her? I am going to my dad's next weekend and I don't know what to do or say. Amber, I really need your advice! I love my mom, but I also really like Cassie. What should I do?

Sincerely,
Torn in Two in Toledo

I wanted them to imagine themselves as Amber, an advice columnist with years of experience. I had them form groups of four and role-play family therapy sessions in which problems are discussed and solutions are sought. In each group, one of them played the family therapist and the others played the roles from one of the Dear Amber letters.

Their writing homework was to choose one of the letters and write a letter of advice back. I told them to specifically answer the questions posed and give supportive reasons for their answers.

The students' writing assignments encapsulated some of the ideas discussed in the groups. Here is one student response.

Dear Torn in Two in Toledo:

Thank you for your letter. I understand your situation because I grew up with both a mother and a stepmother and it wasn't easy. My parents divorced when I was nine. I never liked my stepmother, but you do and I think that you should treasure that relationship, not wreck it by lying and hurting Cassie's feelings. Your mom is obviously jealous and insecure. She probably still loves your dad and is acting like a very immature person. My advice is that you talk to your dad about the conflict that you are having.

See if he can explain your problem to Cassie so she will understand why you lied and caused all this hassle.

Yours truly,
Amber

Exploring a Theme through Role

In most schools, students are aware of some sort of anti-bullying policy, but time and time again the problem surfaces. Drama provides a way for students to get inside the situation and look at it from various viewpoints. It provides students with a way to talk about bullying situations from the safety of role.

I made up the Samara story after I worked in a classroom where I heard from the students about cyber-bullying. I have used the story to do work on anti-bullying in many classrooms of Junior, Intermediate, or Senior students. Here is how I proceed.

First, students assemble in groups of five, and I ask for a volunteer from each group. I call these students to one side of the room and give them each this snippet.

> **Samara's Father**
> I can't stand hearing that she is afraid to go to school. You would think that after all I have taught her about standing up for herself, she would not be in this position now. She has everything she needs—her own room, a cell phone, her own computer for goodness sake. What else could a kid want?

They read the snippet and then I give them this direction: "Assume that the members of your group are going to be playing people who are interested in what you have to say. When you return to the group, adopt the role of Samara's father. Don't read the snippet to the group members but say what he would say in your own words."

I give the students time to look over the snippet again while I talk to the rest of the class. "The volunteer who has left your group is going to return in a few minutes. I have instructed that student to adopt a role and speak in role. I am not going to tell you how to respond except to say that you must listen to this person and respond by asking further questions about his predicament. See how much you can find out about this person's story."

I allow the students to get on with the task and I circulate throughout the room—listening in on the conversations. Typically, the students are very engaged with the task. In order to assess the involvement of the group members, I stop the role-playing and randomly ask members of various groups to stand and tell me what they have learned about this man's story.

- "It seems that he has a daughter named Samara who appears to be having some difficulty at school."
- "The father is very frustrated by his daughter."

- "He feels that he has given her everything and that she will not stand up for herself."

I then call another member from each group over to the side of the room and hand these students this snippet:

> **Samara's Mother**
>
> Samara won't let me call the school. She says that it will just make it worse. I can't stand seeing her this way. She used to be such a happy child. Since she has gone to that new school, things are very different for her. She is so sad all of the time. It does not matter where she is—home, school, at her grandparents', anywhere. She is always quiet and … just sad. Nothing I do or say seems to do any good.

I ask them to return to their groups in role. We repeat the exercise and I allow the mother and father to interact as well as answer questions from the group members.

I then stop the role-playing and ask that the groups "re-play" part of the conversation so the rest of us can hear it. This technique, "Overheard Conversations," is another formative assessment tool I use to see how engaged the students are with the task and what they are saying to one another in role.

Here is some of what has been "played back" to me.

Father: The problem as I see it is that you have always been too protective of the girl. That is why she is in this mess.

Mother: That is unfair. You always blame me when it comes to the difficult things in life.

Student questioner: Could we get back to talking about Samara and what we can do to make her feel that she can return to school?

When some time has passed, I call a third member from each group over to the side of the room. I give this individual the following snippet and the same information that I gave to the mother and the father. I tell the Jodies that they have to make up the story of what happened last term. I give them a few minutes to do that.

> **Jodie—Onlooker**
>
> I know that I should do something about what is happening to Samara, but I have my own difficulties at the moment. I know these kids. They would just turn on me if I interfered and I don't need that after what happened to me last term in this class.

After the role-playing has been going on for some time, I use this assessment strategy: I ask the Jodies to stand and tell the story of their own bullying situation. They speak in role and answer any questions that I pose.

Finally, I call a fourth person, the one who is to play Samara, and then the fifth person, who becomes a student social worker doing her first family counselling session.

For this interview, I ask that the fathers, mothers, and Jodies sit behind an imaginary Plexiglas window so that they can hear everything that Samara tells the social worker, but cannot intervene.

> **Samara**
> What nobody understands is that I can't even get away from them when I get home. They are everywhere. I can't be on my computer because somehow they have figured out my password. They even text-message me. I have not told any of this to Mom or Dad. They would freak and take away my phone. I need it in case something bad happens.

For the summative evaluation, I ask everyone to write in role. The social workers write clinical reports of what they discovered when they interviewed Samara. They need to date and sign their reports. The Samaras write in their diaries and begin their writing in role with "Dear Diary …" The mothers and fathers write letters to their daughter in response to what they heard her say to the social worker. The Jodies write victim impact statements about how the bullying in the school has affected them.

Once all group members complete their writing, I position them one group at a time in the centre of the classroom space. I ask the Samaras to sit on chairs and the Jodies to sit at their feet. The social workers stand beside them, and the parents form a larger circle right by their daughter. As the orchestra leader, I give these directions: "When I touch you on the shoulder I want you to begin reading your writing. As soon as you hear another person reading, you stop and listen to the next voice. If I touch your shoulder again, it means that I want you to continue reading from where you left off. In this way we will be creating a combination of viewpoints and voices that will tell Samara's story in a theatrical, moving way."

Here is part of a transcript of what took place:

S: Dear diary, I cannot tell you how wonderful it was to finally tell someone about my problems.

SW: October 26. I met with Samara today at lunch. She seemed to be in quite a bit of distress …

S: Dear diary, I was worried about telling the social worker about what has been happening to me for the past nine months of my life.

J: I tell the court what it has been like to live in fear of being laughed at 24/7.

M: My darling Samara: How could we have ever known that you were being tormented in this way?

S: Dear diary, At last I feel that I can breathe.

J: I tell the court that bullying is something that eats away at your soul.

F: Dear Samara: I have been insensitive and wrong and I want to tell you how sorry I am for the way that I treated you …

Writing in Role

Writing in role happens when students who have been involved in a role-playing situation write from the perspective of the character that they have been playing. Often, the writing is surprisingly good—students have "lived through" a dramatic moment and are successful at writing for many reasons, as the following sections suggest.

Getting inside the Story

First, students have been physically, emotionally, and intellectually involved in an imagined situation. As a result, they are not only inside the story, but also inside the language of the story. Their perspectives are immediate and visceral. Their thinking and speaking as characters has allowed them to use vocabulary and turns of phrase that they would not use when speaking as themselves. Having experimented with new language forms and registers, they are writing down what they have already thought and spoken.

Three Junior classrooms and I worked with the picture book *Luba: The Angel of Bergen-Belsen*, told to Michelle R. McCann by Luba Tryszynska-Frederick. We had done a drama where Luba meets with the women in the barracks of her concentration camp to convince them that they need to look after the children. I asked the students to write in role as the children to thank Luba for arguing their case and for convincing the other adults to take them in. Here are some of their letters.

Dear Luba,

If we had not met you we would not be alive. Thank you for defending us and helping us not starve to death. We have lost everything. Now we have YOU.

Yours truly,
The children

Dear Luba,

Those women are as scared as we are. They were not very nice at first. Thank you for convincing them to let us stay. We promise to be good and not make any noise. We will not eat much.

The children

Dear Luba,

You are our hero. Now we might have a few more months to live. We worry about the Nazis and what they will do to us if they find out about us. Please protect us forever.

The children

Writing with Purpose

When given authentic contexts for writing—real purposes—students usually go at the task with enthusiasm and confidence. There is no longer the worry that "I don't know what to write about …" Their writing has a purpose—either to propel the story in the drama on or to sum up their characters' understanding or perspective of the event, relationship, or conflict they have just "lived through."

A Grade 7 class and I once worked with the graphic novel *In a Class of Her Own*. We looked at the scene between Ruby's mother and father on the night before Ruby was to attend school. Ruby had been unable to sleep and had come to her parents' room to be comforted. After they put her back to bed, the parents had an argument about the ethics of having a little girl perform such a brave act in the struggle for the rights of Black children to attend any school they want. The students first worked on the script in pairs, then I asked them to write in role in their diaries as either Ruby's mother or father. The following examples show these perspectives.

Ruby's mother

Dear Diary:

Just when I thought that I had convinced Abon of why it was important to stand up for equal rights, I get him in my face one more time. He needs to be strong and stand behind us, not shiver in his boots. He was a brave soldier and won a Purple Heart but you would not know that tonight. I am being brave not only for Ruby but for all of the children who need her to win this fight. Now I am going to sleep. Who knows what tomorrow will bring.

Ruby's father

Dear Diary:

That wife of mine has put my little Ruby in an impossible position. Tomorrow she will have to face angry, racist parents who do not want her to go to a white school. She is only six years old—How can we expect her to survive? When I was in the U.S. Army—even though I fought for my country and won a Purple Heart—I still faced racism every day. I do not want this to happen to my Ruby—she is too young to face this.

Many Forms of Writing in Role

Writing in role can take many forms—reports, diaries, obituaries, signs, proclamations, affidavits, secret messages in code, cartoons, CD images and words, poems, letters, tombstone engravings, court documents, and announcements.

An affidavit is a more unusual form. I worked with teacher candidates on an integrated arts day using the picture book *The Woman Who Outshone the Sun*. As an example of a writing assessment, we drafted an affidavit for group members to complete together and sign. One group's list of four conditions is shown on page 86.

Both writing in role and then reading in role can be very emotional experiences. Students see their words take on enormous significance in the reading aloud, and they witness how the words, when juxtaposed with other voices, have an impact on the audience. Many students achieve a new understanding of the power of language that they have created. For some, it is a turning point in their writing lives.

Objects Can Write in Role

Objects as well as people can write in role.

Objects in a Novel Setting: I worked in a Grade 9 class that was reading *The Wild Children* by Felice Holman. In this story, a young Russian boy named Alex comes down to breakfast one morning to discover that his whole family has been taken away by the GPU—the secret police. The beginning chapter is very dramatic. "People had been disappearing. Everyone knew that. And yet, when Alex came down to breakfast and found his whole family had been taken away—his mother, his father, his younger sister Nadya, and his old grandmother—he couldn't believe it." Because Alex slept in a room that was originally a storage room and hidden away from the rest of the house, he had been overlooked. "When he had come down to breakfast, there wasn't a sign of anyone—no fire in the grate. There was not even the detested smell of scorched oatmeal. But even before that, the first thing that had alerted Alex and had started the wave of fear had been the chair overturned in the front hall."

We worked with tableaux to discover what the moment of attack might have been like for the family. The tableaux told the stories of the interruption of a normal breakfast—one soldier who had grabbed the little girl had taken her piece of toast and was eating it! We then did a soundscape of what Alex might have been able to hear if he had been awake. We decided that the only thing that could tell us the truth of the incident was the overturned chair in the hallway. I asked the students to find a partner and to write from the chair's perspective. Here are two examples. One is a cinquain; one is open verse.

Chair
never used
falling, crashing, tripping
such strong defense against
terror

—Skye and Terri

I have stood
In the hall
For years.
Never noticed.
Never used.

Today I tried
To stop it all from
happening.
As they were dragged
SCREAMING from this hallway
I got in their way.

They did not notice me
                    F
                  A
                L
                  L.

Now I wait for the boy
To wake up
To put our lives back
Together.
Again.

—Meg, Brock and Alvin

Historical Artifacts: The following writing in role came from Grade 8 students working with medals that were introduced as a catalyst for writing about the First World War.

It's World War 1. The whole world has erupted into chaos, gunshots are heard everywhere in the battlefield. A battalion is in confusion as enemy units fire at their trench, missing them narrowly. Suddenly, out of the chaos and confusion emerges a commander, who needs to lead his battalion. Gunshots are fired around him. Soon he reaches the trench and waves his helmet around, as the soldiers see the helmet they pull him into the trench to protect him.

The soldier is badly wounded and needs help. They send for the medics in their battalion and soon two men dressed in white come to the wounded soldier. They take off his jacket. They realize he is a commander.

The commander has been badly injured, but he pushes the medic aside and takes a gun off a dead man and takes a position on the trench. He reloads the gun and fires at the trees where the enemy was hiding. Seeing their commander fighting, they also take up arms and shoot at the trees. Soon the enemy retreats. Then the commander takes out a picture of three people: his son, his wife and himself. Then he closes his eyes.

When the commander opens his eyes he finds his wife holding a baby in her arms. The commander gives a weak smile and goes back to sleep. After some time, the commander goes back home. The doctors complain about him going back, but the commander says he's fine.

At home he gets a warm welcome from his family and friends the next day.

I was awarded to him the next day. I was awarded to him as a sign of courage and valour. After receiving me, he suddenly collapsed. All the people helped him and got him to the hospital. After weary hours the doctors sadly drooped their heads and told his wife he was dead. The weary days passed slowly after his funeral, when I was set in a dark cupboard with no companions. Soon the commander's wife came running upstairs and with trembling hands placed me in a box with a baby bootie and a picture of her parents.

After two days in darkness inside the box I knew I was going to be taken out and I was. I was sent to a lab for research and was shipped to someplace in America. I hope to see the commander's wife again.

—Rapten

Objects Shown in Photographs: These poems resulted from Grade 8 students working with a vivid picture of a dust storm and writing in role from the perspective of objects. The teacher candidate, Amy Sattherthwaite, edited the poems afterwards.

We are her valued objects
we remind
and comfort
her during storms
we live alone in a drawer
we come out during bad times
to help her
if she is
lonely
we are her
past
her
baby
husband
and parents
they are dead
but
to
her
we
are
them

—Owen

I am ashes
I remind her of
the happy days
she had with me.
When she looks at me
she starts to cry
I don't know why but she cries.
She cries for a
couple of hours
she just sits there and cries.
She cries like a baby,
an old baby.
She doesn't only
cry for me, she
cries for my son
who died in the last
duststorm,
she cries a lot for him too.
I am not the
only thing that reminds
her of me.
She also has two pictures of mine.
Well, she used to.
I am her husband's ashes.
I remind her of
her husband.

—Sunny

Role-playing allows us to isolate a particular event or to compare one event to another, to look at events in other places and times and to link them to our own understanding of the world in which we live. It allows us to enter into a story or a character's life, live through that experience, and then emerge with new understandings of the lived experience. It propels us into writing in role—taking on new voices and new perspectives, and responding to imagined realities with confidence, insight, and heightened understanding.

Role-playing and writing in role should be a central feature of any literacy classroom. If you use drama in the classroom, you can introduce an unlimited number of contexts that allow students to safely experience "what that might have been like." Students can play politicians, social workers, historical figures, Shakespearean characters, and people with all sorts of different problems that can be explored and reflected upon both in role and out of role. The excitement that this kind of work generates in the classroom is palpable—students look forward to learning in and through an imaginary experience.

9. Transcripts, Objects, and Artifacts— Constructing Understanding

I am always on the lookout for sources of fascination to students. My goal is to intrigue them, connect to what they are learning, allow them to wonder, encourage them to think in new ways, and thrust them into that delightful place where they want to know more and won't be content until they do.

I encourage you to consider the potential of sources such as these:

- advertisements and personal testimonials;
- documents in the original handwriting or language, for example, journals, letters, and diaries;
- cartoons;
- stories and novel excerpts;
- recipes;
- lists, statistics;
- pictures and postcards, which might trigger recognition in settings for novels and plays;
- paintings;
- video clips and Web pages;
- oral histories;
- interviews;
- music to play while using voice-over techniques or during student presentations;
- audio recordings of famous speeches;
- primary source documents, such as census data, land surveys, maps, ordinances, blueprints, architectural drawings, and transcripts;
- photographs;
- objects and artifacts; and
- picture books, quotes, and poetry, to inspire good questions and critical thought.

The Internet is, of course, invaluable in finding sources. One of my former students always checks out the images on the *Toronto Star* Web site and downloads photographs that could be useful triggers for creative writing.

What Old Photos Can Tell

In my collection, I have old photos of abandoned houses, families, soldiers, action shots of battle, and postcards of faraway places and the way the places looked many years ago. I find many of them on the Internet.

When students look at photographs on an overhead, I ask them to notice facial expressions, relationships, background, foreground, lighting, and dress. What do the photographs tell about the technology, tools, and materials available through time? (For example, take a look at old cars, sewing machines in factories, and weapons in war.) How have the technologies changed? I ask students to study the facial expressions of the people in a photograph, the relationships that seem to exist between them, the setting, the photo's formality or informality. Was the photo staged or did it catch a moment in time? How can the students tell? Photographs can make history come alive.

Dionne Brand's beautiful poem "Blues Spiritual of Mammy Prater" is about a photograph. Once, before introducing the poem, I showed slides of Black families, groups of children, and single Black older women—I had retrieved the images from the Internet after typing in "slave narratives." I then flashed an image of an older Black woman with a white collar in a black dress staring right at the camera. I asked students to look at the picture and write down everything they saw and wondered about this woman. What stories could she tell? What kind of personality did she have? Was she alone or connected to others? What could they imagine about her life? Whom did this person remind them of? Could they connect in any way to this character? What would be her motto? What kind of creed would she live by? What advice would she give to modern young men and women?

Here are two pieces of writing by high-school students responding to the photo:

> I can tell that this woman has lived a life full of personal trials. She has been beaten and trodden on but she has always found a way to stand up again and walk the road—her road—into the future. Her eyes tell of her suffering but they also reveal a certain strength—a kind of knowing that she can survive just about anything. She aches, (you can tell she is still aching) and she is troubled by the world's unfairness, but she keeps on going. Her motto is "I believe."
>
> —Maxwell, Grade 12

> My great aunt has the same kind of attitude as this woman. I only have just met her because she has just arrived in Canada but I see similarities between the two women. They have the same look. The look is not in the eyes but in their bodies—a heavy set-ness that says they will be staying no matter what. They slump and look slightly defeated but they are not leaving. They are going to wait until life gets better. My aunt's motto would be something like, "I waited forever." I think the woman in the photograph is still waiting. She seems determined, patient and strong.
>
> —Silvana, Grade 11

After students wrote in response to the photo source provided, we went on to see how the poet responded to such a photo and to compare perceptions. Brand's words point to the power of well-chosen photographs.

Blues Spiritual for Mammy Prater

On looking at the photograph of Mammy Prater, an ex-slave, 115 years old when her photograph was taken

she waited for her century to turn
she waited until she was one hundred and fifteen
years old to take a photograph
to take a photograph and to put those eyes in it
she waited until the technique of photography was
suitably developed
to make sure that the picture would be clear
to make sure no crude daguerreotype would lose
her image
would lose her lines and most of all her eyes
and her hands
she knew the patience of one hundred and fifteen years
she knew if she had the patience,
to avoid killing a white man
that I would see this photograph
she waited until it suited her
to take this photograph and to put those eyes in it.

in the hundred and fifteen years which it took her to
wait for this photograph she perfected this pose
she sculpted it over a shoulder of pain,
a thing like despair which she never called
this name for she would not have lasted
the fields, the ones she ploughed
on the days that she was a mule, left
their etching on the gait of her legs
deliberately and unintentionally
she waited, not always silently, not always patiently,
for this self-portrait
by the time she sat in her black dress, white collar,
white handkerchief, her feet had turned to marble,
her heart burnished red,
and her eyes.

she waited one hundred and fifteen years
until the science of photography passed tin and
talbotype for a surface sensitive enough
to hold her eyes
she took care not to lose the signs
to write in those eyes what her fingers could not script
a pact of blood across a century, a decade and more
she knew that it would be me who would find
her will, her meticulous account, her eyes,
her days when waiting for this photograph
was all that kept her sane
she planned it down to the day,
the light,

the superfluous photographer
her breasts,
her hands
this moment of
my turning the leaves of a book,
noticing, her eyes.

—Dionne Brand

What Have You Got? Significant Objects

For many years I have used artifacts in my teaching. There is something wonderful about the windows and doors that are opened up in students' imaginations as they are allowed to choose the prop that will enhance the scene, use the object in a series of tableaux to change the meaning and symbolism, or research the way in which the object worked and how the technology has changed over time.

When students are working with a novel or looking at historically significant people, the use of objects or artifacts can help them crystallize their understandings of characters and events; it can also help them articulate their insights, especially if they have to defend their choices. Have the class sit in groups of four or five. Ask students to decide who they want to represent in the novel they are reading or in the historical period they are studying. Invite a volunteer from each group to come to the centre of the room and choose one object from an array of 16 to 20. The students place their chosen articles in their pockets or in handbags and return to their group circles.

After a volunteer withdraws the article and places it on the desk or table for all of a group to see, the group asks three to five questions (typical questions appear in the margin). The volunteer can choose to hide the character's identity or can reveal it immediately. This exercise focuses not on guessing the characters, but on finding out more about their experiences.

When I worked in a Grade 7 History class using this exercise, I volunteered to go first and demonstrated the concept with one group of questioners. I played explorer Jacques Cartier with a quill pen. Notes about the exchange follow.

Why do you have a quill pen? I said that I kept the quill pen so that I could write about my experiences in the New World.

Where do you keep it? I kept the quill pen in my very comfortable quarters beside the ink well.

Are your quarters locked? I told the sailors that no doors are locked on board ship in case of storms. Everyone needs to be on deck and locks could cause a problem especially if the storms were violent.

Aren't you worried about your quill pen being stolen? I was not worried about anyone stealing it because I was one of two men on board ship who could read and write. Most of the sailors were illiterate. I liked it that way because they looked up to me as an educated and intelligent man of letters.

To open up divergent thinking and to encourage students to "warm up their brains," I play a quick game involving objects. Pass the Pencil gets them interacting and is also a great vocabulary building exercise for ESL and ELL students. See Chapter 2 for notes on how to play it.

Own the Object
- What personal significance does this article have for you?
- How do you use it?
- Where do you keep the article? Why?

History comes alive for students who are introduced to primary sources. Using authentic artifacts, documents, photographs, pictures of old tombstones, and manuscripts can enhance your social studies curriculum. The use of historical transcripts is explored later in this chapter.

What if you run out of ink? The Indians had taught me about how to crush berries and I had been successful in creating ink from purple berries that I had found close to the shore.

Who do you think will read your diary? I told the group that all captains have diaries or log books. I said I supposed that the King of France would want a report when I got home so it was good to have notes about my experiences in my diary for reference.

A student volunteered. She chose a leaf from a tree, and in role as Jacques Cartier's First Mate, explained that after the terrible winter when the crew nearly died from scurvy, she began to carry the leaf as a memory of the kindness of the Native people and how they saved their lives. The First Mate keeps it close to the heart because the leaf—like the heart—is a symbol of life.

Unlocking Stories through Object Perspectives

A story circle is composed of five or six students who sit in a circle facing one another. They number off 1, 2, 3, 4, 5, 6. On a signal given by the teacher, the number 1s begin to retell the story that was just read to them. They say one or two sentences before the number 2s take over. The storytelling continues to be shared by the group members, who may pass if they lack confidence, until it is fully told.

Sometimes I give an artifact to the story circle and have the group tell the story from that perspective. (See "Objects Can Write in Role," pages 86 to 89, too.)

Once, when I was working with a Grade 8 class using the picture storybook *The Woman Who Outshone the Sun*, I handed one group the collar of Lucia's dress and the storytellers told Lucia's story from that perspective. One boy began the story with these words, "I feel such a burden of being." I will never forget how powerful that moment was and how his artistry encouraged the other students in the group to continue telling Lucia's tragic story with empathy and thoughtfulness.

When working with Grade 9 students in preparation for Michael Miller's play about Nelson Mandela, *In the Freedom of Dreams*, I placed a large bunch of keys in the centre of the whole-class circle. I asked students to volunteer to come into the middle of the circle to tell Nelson Mandela's story from the perspective of the keys that kept him locked in his cell on Robben Island. Once students had heard many different voices, I asked them to return to their desks to write a story from the keys' perspective. They had to write in the voice of the artifact to Nelson Mandela. Here is one example of the writing that emanated from that exercise.

Every time the jailer jangled the keys in your face and said, "You will be locked up forever" I wanted to scream. I hated having to lock a freedom fighter into a dungeon of darkness. Now I sit in a museum on a shelf behind glass with a porridge bowl and your bible. Tourists come to Robben Island to look at us. I can never forget that I was used by evil to silence good. I have no voice. I feel such shame.

—Wilson, Grade 9

Same Object, Different Meanings

I once worked for a full day with Grades 9 and 10 students on a poetry unit. We were working towards a Readers Theatre performance for that evening, but I decided to begin by using different objects and weaving their discussion about them into an interpretation of "The Sorrow of Sarajevo," one of Goran Simic's powerful poems depicting the devastation of war and its brutal impact on everyday life for ordinary people. (See also Chapter 4 for reference to this poem.) I have done the following exercise countless times.

I divided the class into groups of five and then placed an ordinary object into the middle of each circle. I used an artificial carnation, a contemporary photo of an old woman, a baby bootie, a brooch with missing gems, and a yo-yo. I asked the students to talk to one another about the object before them. What did it remind them of?

On a signal, I stopped the discussion and asked the students to think about a different context. "Suppose," I said, "that you think about the object in a different way and place it in an era of war and destruction. How would the use, symbolism, and meaning of the object change?"

The students discussed ideas in their small groups. The artificial carnation that had reminded them of weddings and graduations, of happy times, now changed to a flower that might be used in a funeral procession. Its symbolism changed from one that depicted new beginnings to one that symbolized the end of life. Students saw it as significant that there was only one bootie and noted that the brooch was missing gems just as when, during a war, the sparkle goes out of people's eyes. The discussion was intoxicating. I was so pleased that these students were able to find such meaning in ordinary objects and to project new interpretations about them in a new context.

I then handed out the poem "The Sorrow of Sarajevo" (see page 36 for the text). I asked the students to read the poem all together as a class and then to circle the objects or nouns in the poem. Then I asked them to talk about how the objects' meaning, use, and symbolism had changed because of the war. Their wide- ranging perceptions once again impressed me. In the large-group discussion, they talked about how the river, once a symbol of life, was now one of death; how the wristwatch on the corpse of the woman reminded them that time marches on despite death and destruction. The discussion then moved on to images of the recent tsunami and Hurricane Katrina. The exercise had opened up a discussion that engaged all the students.

History from Primary Sources

Beyond such intriguing sources as old photos and artifacts, primary source documents, especially those linked to the history students are studying, can open up possibilities for students. There is something exciting about being a witness to an event in history and also to considering those who did not speak and who were too intimidated to speak even when asked. Using written transcripts, students can construct their understanding of the historical context through reading, interpreting, and "playing" with the actual words that were spoken.

I used the following exercise to introduce a theme of child labor and the rise of labor unions to a group of Grade 8 students who were studying Canada: A Changing Society. I began by telling them up front that they were not supposed to understand the text right at the beginning, but that we were going to use the clues from the transcript to get an idea of the time period, the issue that was being investigated, the people involved, and the power struggle that existed between labor, children in society, and the law. The transcript they worked with appears below.

Q. How old are you?
A. Nine and a half years, sir.
Q. Is it optional for you to work overtime?
A. Yes.
Q. Do you go home to dinner?
A. Yes; I go home to dinner at 12 o'clock and I return at 1, and I work from 1 until 6.
Q. If you are late a quarter of an hour do you have an hour taken off of your time?
A. Yes.
Q. Do you know if any girl had anything taken off of her wages for playing while she was supposed to be working?
A. No. I did not hear of any.
Q. Do you know what the amount of the fine was?
A. I could not tell you.
Q. Do you know that she was fined?
A. Yes.
Q. By whom?
A. By the foreman.
Q. You have no idea of the amount of that fine?
A. No.
Q. Do you know what it is for?
A. No. I do not know. It was for fixing her hair, or something of that kind.
Q. Has the foreman used bad language towards the girls, such as cursing and swearing?
A. Yes. I have known him to curse and swear.

Students worked in partners. One decided to be the Questioner and the other the person who answered. They read the transcript once—straight—and then again with the Questioner standing and the person who was answering sitting on a chair. The partners then switched roles. I asked the class these questions:

- Who do you think these characters are?
- When do you think this conversation took place?
- How long ago did this happen?
- Where do you think this conversation took place? Give reasons for your answer.
- Do you have any insights as to who these people might be and why this conversation was recorded?

Next, they began reading the pertinent chapter in the History textbook. Having constructed their own understanding of the time period from investigating a bit of live history, they now had a context for reading about labor unions.

Plead to Read: I asked for a volunteer to read the script out loud with me. The class followed along. Then I got the students to work with partners and read the script, changing roles after one reading. The students were to look for a part in the script where the nine-year-old seems to be uncomfortable with the questioning that was taking place.

Role on the Wall: I drew two figures on the chalkboard: one large and one significantly smaller. I entitled the first one "foreman" and the smaller figure "child worker." I asked the students to come up to the board to write words that would describe the characteristics or feelings of each individual who would work in this mill. We then compared characteristics. In the larger figure, the students wrote the words "powerful," "intimidating," "mean," "trickster," and so on. In the smaller figure, they wrote "vulnerable," "too young to be working," "abused," and the like.

Jot the Gist: We held a discussion about where students thought this conversation took place. Many of them guessed that it could have happened in a courtroom during some kind of enquiry. I told them that the script was indeed a transcript of an Inquiry into Child Labour that took place in 1890—well over a hundred years ago. I then asked the students to fill in a sheet about the who, where, what, when, and why of the scenario.

Freeze the Frame: In groups of six, the students created tableaux of what the mill must have looked like when the foreman was in control of all of the children (see Chapter 7). I tapped one "child" in each tableau on the shoulder and invited him or her to step out of the frame and talk about everyday working conditions in the mill. Afterwards, we analyzed each tableau and generated a list of conditions that would be unacceptable to children and their parents.

Query the Question: I asked the class to make a semi-circle of chairs. They were going to have an opportunity to go back in time to interview the owner of a mill in the 1800s. They were to make a list of questions that they would like to ask. I warned them that the owner did not have to answer any question that was rudely asked so they had to be careful not to anger him. I encouraged them to couch their language in formal ways.

Here is the list that was generated by the class:

What kind of a mill do you operate?
How many employees do you have?
What is the proportion of children to adults in your employ?
What is the age of the youngest child?
Do you give the children breaks during the day?
Are they allowed to eat snacks if they get hungry?
Do you every make them work overtime?
How would you describe the characteristics of your foreman?
Why did you hire him?
How do you feel about child labor?
Does the fact that you are employing eight and nine year-olds in a mill that is dangerous ever bother your conscience?

Teach for Tension: I went into role as the owner of the mill. Throughout the questioning I explained clearly that these children and their families would starve to death if I did not employ them. They might as well learn a trade when they were young so that they could continue to do it all their lives. I was unemotional and matter-of-fact.

Stage the Page: For a culminating task, I asked students, in groups, to prepare arguments to be submitted to the Royal Commission into the Investigation of Child Labour. Pictures of the conditions of the children, excerpts from children's diaries, and parental voices could be used as testimony. Each group was to have a spokesperson to act as the lawyer before the commission.

The literacy requirements for the twenty-first century are many. Not only must students possess an ability to read a wide range of texts, they need to be able to entertain a number of different ideas as they make meaning with the texts that they are reading on the page or on the computer screen. Successful readers know how to make inferences as they read—to go beyond the literal meaning of what they are reading, to examine the implied meanings, and to read between the lines to hypothesize about what the author intended. To do all this, students need time to think. Some might need to work with a partner or in small groups, listening to others talk about what they understand. Other students might need to "see the text" in more concrete ways by handling objects that are connected to the context of the reading. A class might benefit by going into role to experience primary source material from the inside out—to talk as the characters and see the situation and environment described in immediate ways.

As literacy teachers, we need to know how and when to use various teaching techniques to help our students grapple with complex texts that have multiple meanings. We need to make a shift in the kinds of literacy tasks we ask our students to undertake, the kinds of thinking we invite them to do, and the kinds of responses we prompt them to make: they can become literate by talking themselves into understanding and writing to understand as well as be understood.

10. Take Time to Integrate

A human being is made to synthesize all forms of experience into one harmoniously functioning whole. If experience is too incoherent to integrate, we may mentally or physically negate what we can't assimilate ...
—James Moffett and Betty Jane Wagner

Integration allows teachers to find authentic, rather than forced ways of connecting various aspects of the curriculum. Content, knowledge, and understanding can be drawn from one discipline and used to enrich and apply to another. Various aspects of the students' separate subject learning can be brought into a meaningful association through planned projects that carefully and skillfully integrate curriculum areas.

Why Integrate Curriculum

Integration allows us to teach in a way that makes sense to the students. They are encouraged to see different perspectives, connect facts and figures, think critically and imaginatively about ideas, work with materials in a variety of ways, and produce oral, written, artistic, dramatic, and musical pieces in a fashion that has an authentic, real-world feel.

Integration of the curriculum

- connects course content, concepts, and skills;
- stimulates image making both in the mind and on paper, and enhances student learning by involving them in visual, auditory, physical, and emotional ways;
- addresses multiple intelligences or learning styles of the students and allows for greater instruction time to address various ideas;
- develops alternative avenues for expression that are not limited to words and numbers;
- opens alternative approaches for learning, teaching, and communication;
- reduces the number of classroom transitions that happen in the school day; and
- fosters relationships among teaching staff, students, and the community.

One problem in many schools—especially in Intermediate/Senior programs—is fragmentation of knowledge. Schools timetable knowledge to happen in chunks of time in random ways rather than in connected, planned experiences where students are led to personal understanding through discussion, research, questioning, reading, writing, artistic representation and other forms of expression. In some schools, traditional structures, timetables, routines, and relationships are so deeply embedded in the school culture that integration seems to be impossible. In schools where students are taught subjects by specialists on a rotary basis, integration can be a real challenge.

It is important that teachers and administrators understand the benefits of this kind of programming, that they be willing to collaborate, and that they set aside time to meet with their colleagues to decide how to do this work. Integration of some aspects of the curriculum requires lots of planning, organization, scheduling, and co-ordination as well as administrative support. Teachers need to spend time to plan together so that they can rely on each other's expertise to teach the curriculum from various approaches.

I always encourage groups of teachers who are planning an integrated unit to teach from their strengths, but monitor themselves as learners in the process. They need to watch their colleagues teach, ask questions, and set goals and strategies to try themselves. Being able to plan with colleagues and hear what they have to say about what they know so well is informal in-service. It is invaluable for any teacher.

I think that you have to make the decision to teach this way. You need to look carefully at the curriculum and see what can be managed in terms of time and connections; then you need to seek out your colleagues. Work with those who have different sets of knowledge than you. They bring a different perspective and can flesh out the original ideas that you have. The reproducible page "Questions to Guide Planning of an Integrated Unit" may prove useful to you.

Pointers for Planning

Here is some advice about planning an integrated unit:

1. Start from a culminating task and map backwards.
2. Brainstorm all the possibilities.
3. Seek out help from your colleagues.
4. Get support from the school administration.
5. Get in touch with the school librarian to get resources and other ideas. Book the library for several classes.
6. Let the parents and the community know what you are planning. You might want to send a letter to the parents/guardians asking for their help and interest.
7. Negotiate the timelines with your students so that they do not become overwhelmed.
8. Work at integrating subjects, using as many different teaching strategies as you can.
9. Don't force the connections.
10. Keep in mind the different kinds of learning styles in your classroom. Some kids are going to do really well at the research and not so well in the dramatic presentation. How do you support and teach along the way so that kids feel comfortable as well as challenged?

Three examples of successful integrated units follow on pages 104 to 110.

Questions to Guide Planning of an Integrated Unit

If you are meeting with a group of teachers to plan an integrated unit together, keep these questions in mind.

- **Think carefully about all the students you teach.**
  What are the challenges?
  Have you looked at all the learning styles and intelligences in your classrooms?

- **Think about what is expected in terms of standards and expectations.**
  What can you design to interest and challenge everyone?
  What can you design to allow students to become creative, independent learners?

- **Link integration to expectations.**
  What do you want students to know and be able to do by the end of this unit?
  How will you be able to measure what they have learned?
  What kind of performance task can you design to inform you of all of this learning?
  How can you ensure that the judgments you make are fair?

- **Consider timetabling issues.**
  How many subjects can you integrate without forcing the connections?
  What is feasible in terms of time?
  How can you restructure the schedule and timetable?

- **Make the unit personally relevant to students.**
  What kinds of human stories can you find to engage the students?
  What kinds of artifacts can you bring into the classroom and use?
  Who in the community could become a guest speaker?
  What field trips would enhance what is being learned?
  What kind of culminating task would inspire the students to want to know more?

"I Am From …" and Beyond

Since the publication of my book *What Do You Do about the Kid Who …?* I have worked with teachers and students to expand the "I am from …" activity. It has gone from being a getting-to-know-you strategy to more of a literacy experience in which students make decisions about personal information to share with others, as well as literacy choices about text and artistic selections about performance.

Scan the Plan: I tell the students that we are going to examine the kinds of experiences, places, people, relationships, words, images, food, celebrations, sayings, and readings that have shaped who they are and what they are becoming.

Greet the Group: I usually address the class in much this way: "This exercise is going to help you write about who you are, reflect on the kinds of experiences and encounters that have shaped you and your identity, and give you an opportunity to connect with another person in the class. I am going to structure the activity in a certain way so that you work independently first and then with a partner. I would like to encourage you to roam all over the place in your imagination and memory. Feel free to record anything that you think you would like to share about yourself. Don't hesitate to say what you want to say about yourself in a new way. You will have time to work with a partner to change things about your writing so that you can combine your voices and ideas to create a "We are from …" poem.

Jot the Gist: I hand out an index card to each student and encourage them not to talk while they do the activity. First, they write these three words at the top of their cards: **I am from …** Then, modelling the kinds of things I would write about myself, I ask them to record answers to the prompts that I dictate to them:

- What is your favorite thing to eat? (*I am from macaroni and cheese with breadcrumbs on top, fresh out of the oven.*)
- What stores, parks, or landmarks do you pass on the way to school? (*I am from concession roads that go on forever.*)
- Do you have any family sayings? (These can be written in the student's first language.) Describe.
- Is there an old toy or keepsake that you will never throw away?
- Describe where you keep that special item.
- Name the place you wish you could return to when you have more time.
- Think about holiday food, songs, and traditions. Describe them. (*I am from tourtière on Christmas Eve.*)
- Write about daily happenings. (*I am from socks that will not stay up.*)
- Describe memories of people you love.
- In what places do you feel safe and loved? (*I am from French mingled with English.*)
- Is there anything else that you would like to tell?

Tinker with Text: Have the students find a partner and share their "I am from …" poems." Give them 10 to 15 minutes to share what each line means. You will find that they have lots to tell one another.

Now, invite them to combine their poems so that their voices and the words, images, and meanings work together to make a "We are from …" poem.

Encourage them to change words, delete lines, add more poetic language, speak lines and words chorally, layer sound, include sound effects, pause for effect, and repeat images. Have them add lines that give more information in artistic ways.

Here is a good poem that two first-year teachers composed together quickly in one of my workshops. It reflects their combined experiences.

We are from …
… schools and churches, parks and games;
We are from …
… Sunday night barbeques and Bubba's at Yankee Stadium.
We are from …
… "Sonny, What are you doing?" And "Tell Someone who cares."
We are from …
… Lazy Lake Nippissing and the Mattawa River
… Old photo albums rarely enjoyed
… My son's first snow boots, right up there on the shelf.
… My Mom's careful worrying and my dad's beginning belief in who I am.

Plead to Read: Have the students read their poems to another set of partners. The partners can give critical feedback. They might suggest words that can be changed or repeated, or different turns of phrase. If they wish to, let students read their poems in front of the class.

Stage the Page: My most successful work with this exercise happened when I encouraged some Grade 11 students to bring in a prop or a costume piece to augment their joint reading. I then asked them to think of a way to "stage the page." Where could this reading take place? How could they physically represent the meaning of the poem? Some students asked others in the class to help in the staging of the poem. One group staged their reading in a refugee camp, another at a large family reunion, and another at an airport departure lounge. Some students decided to play music to introduce their piece. Others brought in instruments and asked their friends to play a note at a significant time in the performance. Some students began their reading with recorded music that continued softly throughout the performance.

After we had shared the duos, I asked student pairs to pick their favorite lines, to write them on a sheet of paper, and to put them in a hat. The class was divided into three groups, and each group worked with the lines to come up with a "We are from …" poem that they could edit to make something that worked artistically and theatrically. Each group had to find a way to stage the page: they could use music, song, props, costumes, and so on. They were allowed to "borrow lines" from other groups to make their poems work. Their culminating task was to do a choral reading of their poem in a school assembly. Their teacher, Bleema Getz, worked with them to create the class poem.

Here is one result.

We are from a world constantly changing
A hard world, a big world, a get-up-and-get-go world.
Where once we saw rivers moving with flawless flow
And coconuts cracking in the hot summer sun
We now see a dark cityscape of crime and drugs
We are from families who work hard to protect us
Descendants of general commanders and business women
Who forbid us to fail.

Our lives echo with sayings
"Don't do what I did." "You have the chance I never had."
Carved over all of our features
Are street lights in winter
Presents under a tree
Soccer at lunch
And a songbird that spreads the magic of her voice on our hearts.

One of these students created an especially powerful "I Am From ..." poem on his own. Note how he does not begin the first and last stanzas with that phrase, but plays with I, A, M, F, R, O, M, in the first and last stanzas.

I Am From

In times of violence, poverty and crime
As days go by we get closer to the end of time
My heart is beating loud and fast
Fire burns inside me when I remember the past
Reality gets false and fiction gets more real
Only those who analyze
Maybe, they will realize the true deal.

I am from playing soccer at lunch or after school with most of my friends
I am from all types of music but mostly rock and metal; they make me feel good when I'm stressed;
I am from fried chicken, most kinds of fruits, mild and all Colombian food.
I am from Ossington to Dufferin station every morning and Dufferin mall at lunch or after school;
I am from a family that will always welcome me and will always be happy to see me
I am from studying history and looking at maps of the world, I think of how one day it will change;
I am from talking about wrestling, soccer, music, the world, martial arts, history and other stuff with some of my friends;
I am from a place that most people don't really know about, a country full of shadow caused by violence and drugs, the land of the best coffee in the world, my favourite place on earth, the country where I was born. I am from Colombia.

I feel irrational, so confrontational
And I think my thoughts and I don't even want to
My soul is in a comma and nobody can tell
Foreseeing the future I try to get
Ready to get faster, smarter and stronger
Only if I want to survive any longer
My body feels sick and tired of being sick and tired.

—Bernardo

A Balanced Literacy Unit Based on a Story

"The Choice" earlier appeared in *Variations Literature Program: Shadowbox Anthology,* published by Harcourt, Brace & Jovanovich, 1976.

The story that provides the basis for this model is "The Choice," written by Wayland Young.

Before Williams went into the future he bought a camera and a tape-recording machine and learned shorthand. That night, when all was ready, we made coffee and put out brandy and glasses against his return.

"Good-by," I said, "Don't stay too long."

"I won't," he answered.

I watched him carefully, and he hardly flickered. He must have made a perfect landing on the very second he had taken off from. He seemed not a day older; we had expected he might spend several years away.

"Well?"

"Well," said he, "let's have some coffee."

I poured it out, hardly able to contain my impatience. As I gave it to him I said again, "Well?"

"Well, the thing is, I can't remember."

"Can't remember? Not a thing?"

He thought for a moment and answered sadly, "Not a thing."

"But your notes? The camera? The recording-machine?"

The notebook was empty, the indicator of the camera rested at "1" where we had set it, the tape was not even loaded into the recording-machine.

"But good heavens," I protested, "why? How did it happen? Can you remember nothing at all?"

"I can remember only one thing."

"What was that?"

"I was shown everything, and I was given the choice whether I should remember it or not after I got back."

"And you chose not to? But what an extraordinary thing to—"

"Isn't it?" he said. "One can't help wondering why."

—Wayland Young

Greet the Group: When I do this integrated unit with students, I don't give them much information. I hand out lined index cards and ask them to list the following items: personal identification, oxygen mask, food and water, digital camera, diary or log book, current statistics of the world's population, newspaper, change of clothing, first aid kit, tape recorder, history book, map of the world, pocket mirror, diamonds and gold, computer, video camera, matches, and weapon.

Teach for Tension: Then I say: "You have an opportunity to go into the future. You are allowed to take only three items on the list with you. Each of you makes your own choice."

There are always questions, for example: How far into the future are we going? How will we get there? Will we be coming back? I mention travel is by time machine, but other than that, I say I am unsure. After the students have spent time making their choices, they work with a partner trying to come to a consensus on which three items they would like to take. This discussion allows students to defend their choices and leaves room for them to think about other perspectives and change their minds. We have a whole-class discussion about what people think. Kids usually have strong feelings about what items they should take into the future.

Make Machines: A few years ago I worked with a group of boys (Grades 4–8) at a conference on boys and literacy. A huge number of boys from Boys Reading Clubs across the city and I found ourselves working in a confined space in a hotel conference room. The boys were bursting with energy and very interested in what we were doing, so I asked them to make time machines in small groups. They happily created amazing time machines with their bodies and voices. A spokesperson for each group explained how the machine worked and each machine was brought to life. I was impressed by the sophistication of the boys' language as they described intricate details of their machines.

Plead to Read: After we shared the machines, I read aloud Wayland Young's "The Choice."

Freeze the Frame: I asked the question: What did Williams see in the future and why did he choose not to remember? In groups, the boys created tableaux that told this part of the story. We looked at each tableau and I asked the workshop participants to take a good long look at the tableaux and tell me more of the story.

Write in Role: The boys then wrote in role as Williams—describing what they had seen and why they had made the decision not to remember the future.

Geography in the Shoes of an Icon

As recorded in Chapter 1, my pre-service candidates settled on Terry Fox as an engaging way to enter study of the geography of Canada. The challenge then became how to create a unit in which everyone would want to take a part. What follows are suggestions on how to proceed.

Freeze the Frame: Suggest that students find out some information about Terry Fox's run across the country to Thunder Bay. Here are seven excerpts from the journey, documented on **www.terryfoxrun.org/english/marathon/timeline**. Students in groups could locate one of the towns or cities on a map and create a tableau that encapsulates the event in that city.

April 12: 0 km St. John's, NF Terry Fox dips his artificial leg into the Atlantic Ocean and sets out on his *Marathon of Hope*.

May 15: 1278 km Sheet Harbour, NS After a reception where Terry ran with some school children, he wrote: "When I ran with the kids I really burned it just to show them how fast I could go. They were tired and puffing. All right!"

May 26: 1728 km Charlottetown, PEI "There were lots of people out to cheer me on and support me. Incredible! … I had another dizzy spell during the Run. Still freezing, but I wasn't wearing sweats so people could see my leg. I'd run just over twenty-eight miles."

June 6: 2214 km Bristol, NB "The first few miles were the usual torture. My foot was blistered bad, but my stump wasn't too bad. Today I had tremendous support. Everybody honked and waved. People all over looked out of their homes and stores and cheered me on."

June 23: 2917 km Montreal, QC Terry ran into Montreal with Montreal Alouette kicker Don Sweet and four wheelchair athletes.

August 18: 4901 km Wawa, ON The Montreal River Hill, just south of Wawa, is 3 km long. Those who knew it were making the analogy of the hill being Goliath and Terry being David. Terry's t-shirt that day read: *Montreal River Here I Come*, with *I've Got You Beat* on the back!

Sept 1: 5373 km Thunder Bay, ON "People were still lining the road saying to me, "Keep going, don't give up, you can do it, you can make it, we're all behind you." Well, you don't hear that and have it go in one ear and out the other, for me anyway … There was a camera crew waiting at the three-quarter mile point to film me. I don't think they even realized that they filmed my last mile … people were still saying, 'You can make it all the way, Terry.' I started to think about those comments in that mile, too. Yeah, I thought, this might be my last one."

Thunder Bay, ON—Press Conference "That's the thing about cancer. I'm not the only one, it happens all the time to people. I'm not special. This just intensifies what I did. It gives it more meaning. It'll inspire more people … I just wish people would realize that anything's possible if you try. When I started this Run, I said that if we all gave one dollar, we'd have $22 million for cancer research, and I don't care, man, there's no reason that isn't possible. No reason."

Stage the Page: Have the groups work their information into a documentary kind of reportage. They could pursue any of these options:

- playing the role of eyewitnesses and reporters who saw or met Terry at these particular places and create on-the-spot interviews;
- creating artifacts that people might have given him as he ran—these could have written explanations attached to them (e.g., "Hi Terry: Thought you might like to have this jeweled heart—to give you hope and inspiration as you run");
- writing notes of encouragement;
- adding writing to the pages of his diary about the places he most enjoyed;
- creating postcards—on one side, is a picture of an important landmark; on the other, words of encouragement or information that Terry learned about the places he visited and people he encountered.

Other Possibilities

My pre-service candidates thought that students could create a Trip Tick for Terry and his supporters of those places in the rest of Canada that Terry never saw and only imagined. The Trip Tick could recommend places for him to see, people he might like to meet, food he should eat to give him strength, and clothes that he might consider buying to help him deal with the weather and the landscape.

As a culminating task, my pre-service teachers imagined a screening in which the documentary of Terry Fox's life is presented. They thought that they could have students, in groups of six, stage a part of Terry's story—the focus would be on Terry with information about the country that he began to know so well as the backdrop. The class could put together a ceremony of remembrance, where each province and territory is represented by a delegation that tells the story of Terry Fox—what he experienced and what he missed.

For many students, geography will come to life when a story can teach them the information they need to know. Terry Fox is an icon—his travels, his cancer, and his courage link together to tell us amazing stuff about the human spirit. Canadian geography is the backdrop—but it is a huge part of the story.

I always look for the *big* stories of life—ones that can help us learn about new places, experience different perspectives, encounter people we would not find in our own environments. Stories can create magic and a sense of wonder in the classroom. Storytelling linked to subjects such as history, science, and geography provide unique ways for us to integrate the curriculum—to broaden it—so that students develop an understanding, respect, and appreciation for other cultures, places, people, and their ideas.

Final Words: One Eye on Reality, Another on Possibility

One looks back with appreciation to the brilliant teachers, but with gratitude to those who touched our human feelings. The curriculum is so much necessary raw material, but warmth is the vital element for the growing plant and for the soul of the child.
—Carl Jung

In May 2006, I finished an exciting project where I worked with the Canadian Education Association and 27 Grade 12 students from Vancouver, Halifax, and Toronto (nine from each city.) Under my direction, the students researched, created, and performed a drama collective called "Imagine a School ..." at the symposium "Getting It Right for Adolescent Learners" in Vancouver, British Columbia.

The students and I had only a few months to research and write a play that would have an impact on the decisions of Canadian educational leaders, such as directors and senior superintendents. We initially worked all together at "Destination Arts," York University, and then in small groups in the three cities. Finally, we had a short rehearsal period in Vancouver where we put the play together. The students opened the conference with their hour-long anthology. When it was over, the audience stood, applauded, cheered, and wept.

The student scenes told different stories of schooling from many perspectives, but from this pan-Canadian student collective came several common messages. One key message from the students was simply, "Teach us." There was a universal cry for interesting, open-ended, relevant, and imaginative teaching.

And teach we will. Yes, we may encounter rough waters as we strive to become excellent teachers, creating open-ended literacy tasks responsive to our students' needs and interests. The journey to imaginative teaching and joyful learning is full of interruptions, tentative discoveries, negative attitudes, lack of resources, and questioning by colleagues. I believe, however, that the work is worth all the disappointments, self-doubt, and worry. Initially, our rewards will be small —the glimmer of understanding, the thankful parent phone call—but these will be followed by the students' excitement about their projects and finally their triumphs in understanding and comprehension. They will have leapt into literacy and will find themselves part of the club of educated people who think, speak, and write with an understanding of audience, of the power of metaphor, of the subtlety of nuance, and of the importance of voice.

As William Ayers has written so beautifully,

Humanistic teachers need to develop an entirely different rhythm, sometimes in the cracks and crevices of the classrooms we are given. We begin with a many-eyed approach: an eye on your students and an eye on yourself, an eye on the environment for learning and an eye on the contexts within which your work is embedded. You need an eye on reality and another on possibility.

You might end each day asking, "What didn't I do well today? Could I have done better with this student or that one? What alternatives exist?" And you might start the next day forgiving yourself for your lapses and shortcomings, ready to start again. Without self-criticism, teachers can become too easily satisfied, and then self-righteous. But without acceptance they are vulnerable to self-loathing, to berating themselves unnecessarily. Criticism and forgiveness—this is the path to wisdom in teaching. We are, each one of us, a work-in-progress. We are pilgrims who see our students as unruly sparks of meaning-making energy on a voyage through their lives. We, too, are on a journey. Let's create a teaching life worthy of our teaching values.

Personal Ways to Respond to Reading

I think … _____

I wonder … _____

I feel … _____

I imagine … _____

I know … _____

I predict … _____

I find … _____

I suspect … _____

I admire … _____

I like … _____

I don't like … _____

I was impressed by … _____

I was surprised … _____

I noticed that … _____

I know it is hard to believe but … _____

If I had been there, I would have … _____

The part I don't understand is … _____

The part about _____ reminds me of _____

My favorite part is … _____

The most exciting part is _____ because _____

A part that I find confusing is … _____

If I were the author, I would change … _____

I am most like the character _____ because _____

An interesting word / sentence / idea is … _____

I thought it was funny when … _____

I can relate to this chapter / story / character because … _____

The part that makes a real picture in my mind is … _____

The part that made me angry was … _____

A Tool for Self-Assessment

My writing:

❏   My writing is getting clearer.

❏   I am writing more.

❏   I am becoming more adventurous in my writing.

❏   I am paying more attention to detail.

❏   I am aware of some of the strategies that are helping me write.

My reading:

❏   My reading is becoming more fluent.

❏   I am reading more.

❏   I am reading different kinds of texts.

❏   I am talking about what I am reading.

❏   I am encouraging others to read what I have read.

❏   I am always on the lookout for more to read.

❏   I am aware of some of the strategies that are helping me read.

I am becoming aware of how I learn.

❏   I find that if I can make pictures in my head, I ...

❏   I find that if I can talk about information before I write, I ...

❏   I find that if I wonder aloud first, then ...

❏   I find it most difficult to concentrate and stay on task when ...

I am becoming more confident as I work in groups.

❏   I am trying on different roles in group situations.

❏   If I disagree, I am able to tell people why.

❏   I am learning not to interrupt.

❏   I am trying to be patient.

❏   I work hard to stay on topic.

❏   I am learning how to be diplomatic.

A Tool for Self-Assessment, *cont'd*

I am connecting my learning to ...

❑ other things we are learning in class

❑ things that I knew before

❑ questions that I am writing down

❑ what I am experiencing in my life

I am remembering to ...

❑ date all of my work

❑ hand in my homework

❑ ask if I do not understand

❑ seek help from dictionaries, a thesaurus, my friends, teachers, and others

❑ watch the way that I interact with others

❑ notice people and note events and things that are happening around me

Reflecting on Experiences in Groups

By yourself or with a partner respond to the prompts below. You may also use the back of the page.

Describe a group experience that you found very positive.

_____

_____

Why do you think the group functioned well?

_____

_____

Describe a group experience that was not successful.

_____

_____

What do you think the group did not do so well?

_____

_____

Are you someone who likes to work in a group? Why?

_____

_____

What strengths do you bring to the group?

_____

_____

What weaknesses do you have in a group setting?

_____

_____

How do you behave if the group functioning begins to break down?

_____

_____

What kinds of new roles would you like to try?

_____

_____

Assessment of Work Done in Groups

Name: _____   Group members: _____

_____

Rating scale: (1 is low; 5 is high)

Rate your participation/attendance in the planning of the group assignment

1   2   3   4   5

List the special tasks you completed for the group.

_____

_____

_____

Rate the group process.

1   2   3   4   5

Briefly list the factors that made the group function the way that it did.

_____

_____

_____

Rate your group's final product.

1   2   3   4   5

List any special contributions you made so that the product looked the way that it did.

_____

_____

_____

Describe any insights that you gained about the work that you did.

_____

_____

_____

Choral Reading: Sample Poem

This poem by Jennifer Albert is recommended for choral reading as described in Chapter 5.

Don't I Have a Voice?
Change my clothes
Fix my hair
Why change my world
To fit into theirs?
Why can't they see
What they're doing to me?
It's killing me inside
I'm thinking, "Why me?"

Chorus:
Changing who I am
Don't I have a choice?
Can't I be myself?
Don't I have a voice?

Teased because they
Don't understand me.
If I were to change
What would my life be?
Would I forget my country?
Could I forget my friends?
Leave my life behind me
All its turns and bends.

Repeat Chorus

Drowning in suggestions
Buried in advice
Wouldn't a vote of confidence
Just about now be nice?
Buy new clothes?
Put on makeup?
Sorry I don't think
I need the help.

Repeat Chorus

I am who I am
It's all I can be
Maybe one day
One day they will see
That despite of them
I am still strong
Maybe one day
I'll say they were wrong.
One day I will
Yes one day I will
Because I found my voice.

Story Theatre

Aspects of Story Theatre

- The story is read aloud or delivered from memory.

- Actors must read narrator and character lines.

- Actors "fill out" the narration with improvised action.

- Actors bring the story to life.

Options

- There could be one narrator throughout.

- Each character could take his or her own narration as well as dialogue.

- One group could be narrator, one group could read dialogue, and another group could do actions.

- One player could take more than one role.

- More than one player could take a single role.

Props and Costumes

- Props and costumes should be simple and suggestive. Possible props include books, dolls, old photographs, canes, jewellery, purses, suitcases, tickets, keys, flowers, medals, and paintbrushes/palettes; possible costumes include hats, scarves, gloves, shawls, jackets, uniforms, and aprons.

Sources

- The best source material for Story Theatre is simple, narrative stories such as myths. Legends, fables, folktales, or any strong story that calls for action, movement, and dramatic animation will work well.

Wonder Machines

You are a group of scientists who have decided to design a Wonder Machine that will make the world a better place. You have been invited to present your Wonder Machine at an international conference.

Please identify your group members:

_____

_____

_____

In your group, brainstorm the environmental concerns that exist today and discuss them.

List the five most pressing problems identified by your group.

_____

_____

_____

By consensus, choose one problem that you, as a group of expert scientists, can rectify by inventing an amazing machine.

_____

_____

_____

Decide what kind of mechanism can be created to correct this major world problem.

_____

_____

_____

Put together a machine using movement and voice. Rehearse so that the movements are synchronized and everyone understands what the machine is producing, how it is powered, and how each section fits in with others.

Appoint a spokesperson to present the machine at the International Conference on World Issues. As a group, help the spokesperson create a PowerPoint presentation that can be used during or after the machine's demonstration. You may use images as well as text.

Make a booklet that describes your presentation.

The Expert Game—Oral Language Interview Snapshot Assessment Checklist

Group 1

Student Name	Role	Listens to Others	Projects into Role	Maintains the Role	Builds on Each Other's Questions	Makes Inferences	Synthesizes Information	Speaks in Small Groups	Forms an Opinion
	Expert								
	Interviewer								
	Interviewer								
	Interviewer								

Group 2

Student Name	Role	Listens to Others	Projects into Role	Maintains the Role	Builds on Each Other's Questions	Makes Inferences	Synthesizes Information	Speaks in Small Groups	Forms an Opinion
	Expert								
	Interviewer								
	Interviewer								
	Interviewer								

Group 3

Student Name	Role	Listens to Others	Projects into Role	Maintains the Role	Builds on Each Other's Questions	Makes Inferences	Synthesizes Information	Speaks in Small Groups	Forms an Opinion
	Expert								
	Interviewer								
	Interviewer								
	Interviewer								

Group 4

Student Name	Role	Listens to Others	Projects into Role	Maintains the Role	Builds on Each Other's Questions	Makes Inferences	Synthesizes Information	Speaks in Small Groups	Forms an Opinion
	Expert								
	Interviewer								
	Interviewer								
	Interviewer								

From Talk to Writing: Amber's Advice Column

Choose one of the three letters and respond in writing as if you are Amber, an experienced advice columnist.

Dear Amber:

My son and his wife came by last night to tell my wife and me that they were getting a divorce. Everything has seemed fine between them so it came as a huge shock. We are very sad for them and for their children—two boys and a girl, all under the age of 10.

My daughter-in-law told us that she had been given a promotion at work which means that she will be moving to another state and taking the children with her. This is not too bad for my son because he travels a lot and will be able to see his children quite regularly. The kids will come to stay with him every other Thanksgiving and every other Christmas but they will go to camp in the summer (as they usually do) and will not be coming here for long stays at all.

Amber, my wife and I are devastated because we realize that our daily visits with our grandchildren will be coming to an end. We have been the main caregivers to all of the children for all of their lives because my son and daughter-in-law have worked full time since each child was born. They have high-powered jobs and make a lot of money. The kids come here after school and stay till their parents pick them up, and they sleep over regularly on weekends. We have special, special times together. They love us dearly and we adore them.

What has angered us the most was that my son and his wife were surprised when we told them that we were extremely upset that our feelings were not taken into account when all the decisions about visiting etc. were discussed. We have been left out of the equation and are furious. When we confronted them, they coolly said that divorce was not about us and that we should make the best of it. How should we respond?

Sincerely,

Devastated in Des Moines

Dear Amber:

I am 14 years old and my father has recently remarried. His new wife's name is Cassie and she is funny, kind, and lets me have my friends over on weekends to watch movies and hang out. She also allows me try on her clothes and experiment with her make-up. We talk a lot and get along really well. Actually, she is more like a friend than a stepmother.

The problem is that when I go home after a weekend spent with Cassie and my dad, my mom gets all moody if I tell her anything positive. She bombards me with questions about Cassie and then gets mad if I say anything about her. It's got so that I am beginning to tell her lies about Cassie so that she won't be so jealous. I am beginning to make Cassie out to be something mean and horrible just to make my mom feel better.

The other night I was telling her a stupid lie about something that Cassie had said and my mom got really mad and overprotective and phoned Cassie up and started yelling at her over the phone. I could not get her to stop. It ended with Cassie hanging up on her. Now Cassie knows that I have been telling lies about her. She must be really hurt.

What do I say to Cassie the next time I see her? I am going to my dad's next weekend and I don't know what to do or say. Amber, I really need your advice! I love my mom, but I also really like Cassie. What should I do?

Sincerely,

Torn in Two in Toledo

From Talk into Writing: Amber's Advice Column, *cont'd*

Dear Amber:

I have an older brother named Dave who does really well at school and seems to have the perfect life. He is good looking, funny, popular, and athletic, and has a beautiful girlfriend that my parents really like. He is going to be a business major in college and has just received two scholarships—one academic, the other athletic. I, on the other hand, am quite small for my age and like to spend a lot of time alone. I like to read, watch movies, and play on the computer.

I know that they don't mean to do it, but my parents are always comparing me to Dave. They sometimes catch themselves doing this in front of others, and when they do, they immediately stop talking. All of us, including me, are embarrassed when this happens.

I am fond of Dave, but I don't want to be like him. I like who I am. I am not a genius but I do okay in school and I want to travel and see the world before I go to college. I am interested in animals and habitats and might become a veterinarian or a biologist, but I am not sure right now. The problem is that I feel really insecure when I am with my parents and Dave. They make me think that I am not as good as Dave and sometimes seem really disappointed in me. Often I see them looking at each other in frustration when I do not respond the way Dave might have. Sometimes, I seriously think that I should just move out and live by myself. What do you think?

Sincerely,

Doubting in Detroit

Recommended Resources

Allen, Janet. 2000. *Yellow Brick Roads: Shared and Guided Paths to Independent Reading 4–12*. Portland, ME: Stenhouse.

Atwell, Nancy. 1987. *In the Middle: Writing, Reading and Learning with Adolescents*. Portsmouth, NH: Boynton/Cook.

Atwood, Margaret. 2003. *Oryx and Crake*. Toronto: McClelland & Stewart.

Ayers, William. 2004. *Where We Might Begin with Teaching*. Milwaukee, WI: Rethinking Schools.

Barton, Bob, and David Booth. 1990. *Stories in the Classroom*. Markham, ON: Pembroke.

Booth, David. 2005. *Story Drama: Creating Stories Through Role Playing, Improvising, and Reading Aloud*. Markham, ON: Pembroke.

Booth, David. 2002. *Even Hockey Players Read: Boys, Literacy and Learning*. Markham, ON: Pembroke.

Booth, David, and Larry Swartz, eds. 2004. *Literacy Techniques for Building Successful Readers and Writers*, 2nd ed. Markham, ON: Pembroke.

Booth, David W., and Charles J. Lundy. 1985. *Improvisation: Learning Through Drama*. Toronto: Harcourt Brace Jovanovich.

Booth, David W., and Jonothan Neelands, eds. 1998. *Writing in Role: Classroom Projects Connecting Writing and Drama*. Hamilton, ON: Caliburn Enterprises.

Booth, David W., and Kathleen Gould Lundy. 2006. *In Graphic Detail*. Toronto: Rubicon Publishing.

Brand, Dionne. 1998. *No Language Is Neutral*. Toronto: McClelland & Stewart.

Bruner, J. S. 1986. *Actual Minds; Possible Worlds*. Cambridge, MA: Harvard University Press.

Calkins, Lucy McCormick, and Shelley Harwayne. 1991. *Living Between the Lines*. Portsmouth, NH: Heinemann.

Cambourne, Brian. 1988. *The Whole Story: Natural Learning and the Acquisition of Literacy in the Classroom*. Auckland, AU: Ashton Scholastic.

Christiansen, Linda. 2000. *Reading, Writing and Rising Up: Teaching About Social Justice and the Power of the Written Word*. Milwaukee, WI: Rethinking Schools.

Clay, Marie M. 1993. *An Observation Survey of Early Literacy Achievement*. New York: Heinemann.

D'Arcangelo, Marcia. 1998. "The Brains Behind the Brain." *Educational Leadership* 56 (November): 20–25.

Delpit, Lisa. 2006. *Other People's Children. Cultural Conflict in the Classroom*. New York: The New Press.

Elkind, David. 1981. *The Hurried Child: Growing Up Too Fast Too Soon*. Reading, MA: Perseus Publishing.

Eisner, Elliot. 2002. *The Arts and Creation of Mind*. New Haven, CT: Yale University Press.

Fleischman, Paul. 1997. *Joyful Noise: Poems for Two Voices*. New York: Harper and Row Publishers.

Freire, Paulo. 2001. *Pedagogy of Freedom: Ethics, Democracy and Civic Courage*. New York: Rowman and Littlefield Publishers.

Frost, Helen. 2001. *When I Whisper, Nobody Listens: Helping Young People Write About Difficult Issues*. New York: Heinemann.

Gallagher, Kathleen. 2000. *Drama Education in the Lives of Girls.* Toronto: University of Toronto Press.

Gardner, H. 1983. *Frames of Mind: The Theory of Multiple Intelligences.* New York: Basic Books.

George, Jean Craighead. 2003. *Julie of the Wolves.* Toronto: HarperCollins.

Ghosh, Ratna. 2002. *Redefining Multicultural Education,* 2nd Edition. Toronto: Thomson Nelson.

Golding, William. 1954. *Lord of the Flies.* New York: Simon and Schuster.

Golman, David. 1995. *Emotional Intelligence.* New York: Bantam Books.

Graham, Carolyn. 1979. *Jazz Chants.* Toronto: Oxford University Press.

Graves, D. H. 1994. *A Fresh Look at Writing.* Portsmouth, NH: Heinemann.

Greene, Maxine. 2001. *Variations on a Blue Guitar. The Lincoln Center Institute Lectures on Aesthetic Education.* New York: Teachers College Press.

Heathcote, Dorothy, Cecily O'Neill, and Liz Johnson, eds. 1991. *Dorothy Heathcote: Collected Writings on Education and Drama.* Evanston, IL: Northwestern University Press.

Hehner, Barbara, ed. 1999. *The Spirit of Canada: Canada's Story in Legends, Fiction, Poems and Songs.* Toronto: Malcolm Lester Books.

Heschel, Abraham. 1996. *Moral Grandeur and Spiritual Audacity.* Essays edited by Susannah Heschel. New York: Farrar, Strauss and Giroux.

Hollis, Matthew, and Paul Kegan, eds. 2003. *101 Poems Against War.* New York: Faber and Faber.

Johnson, David W., and Frank P. Johnson. 1991. *Joining Together: Group Theory and Group Skills.* Needham Heights, MA: Allyn and Bacon.

Koechlin, Carol, and Sandi Zwaan. 2001. *Info Tasks for Successful Learning: Building Skills in Reading, Writing and Research.* Markham, ON: Pembroke.

Kohl, Herbert R. 1998. *Discipline of Hope: Learning from a Lifetime of Teaching.* New York: Simon and Schuster.

Konigsburg, E. L. 2000. *Silent to the Bone.* New York: Atheneum Books for Young Readers.

Lundy, Charles, and David Booth. 1985. *Interpretation: Working with Scripts.* Toronto: Harcourt Brace Jovanovich.

Lundy, Kathleen Gould, Christine Jackson, Lorna Wilson, and Lorraine Sutherns. 2001. *The Treasure Chest: Story, Drama and Dance/Movement in the Classroom.* Toronto: Toronto District School Board.

Maritinez, Alejandro Cruz. 1991. *The Woman Who Outshone the Sun. La Mujer que brillaba aun mas que el sol.* San Francisco: Children's Book Press.

McIntosh, P. 2000. "White Privilege: Unpacking the Invisible Knapsack." In *Gender Through the Prism of Difference,* 2nd Edition, edited by M. B. Zinn, P. Hondagneu-Sotelo, and M. A. Messner, pp. 247–50. Boston: Allyn and Bacon.

Moffett, James, and Betty Jane Wagner. 1992. *Student-Centered Language Arts, K–12.* Portsmouth, NH: Heinemann/Boynton Cook.

Morgan, Norah, and Juliana Saxton. 2006. *Asking Better Questions,* 2nd Edition. Markham, ON: Pembroke.

Neelands, Jonothan. 1984. *Making Sense of Drama: A Guide to Classroom Practice.* London: Heinemann.

Neelands, Jonothan. 1992. *Structuring Drama Work.* Cambridge: Cambridge University Press.

Pally, R. 1997. "How the Brain Development Is Shaped by Genetic and Environmental Factors." *International Journal of Psycho-Analysis* 78: 587–93.

Paterson, Katherine. 1988. Gates *of Excellence. On Reading and Writing Books for Children.* New York: E. P. Dutton.

Pennac, Daniel. 1994. *Better Than Life.* Markham, ON: Pembroke; Portland, ME: Stenhouse.

Raczka, Bob. 2002. *No One Saw. Ordinary Things Through the Eyes of an Artist.* Brookfield, CT: Millbrook Press.

Rigby, Ken. 2001. *Stop the Bullying: A Handbook for Teachers.* Markham, ON: Pembroke.

Rigg, Kate. 2003. "The Phoenix Rides a Skateboard." In *Shakin' the Stage,* edited by Glenda MacFarlane. Toronto: Scirocco Drama.

Styles, Donna. 2001. *Class Meetings: Building Leadership, Problem-Solving and Decision-Making in the Respectful Classroom.* Markham, ON: Pembroke.

Schwartz, Susan, and Maxine Bone. 1995. *Retelling, Relating, Reflecting: Beyond the 3Rs.* Toronto: Irwin Publishing.

Schniedewind, N., and E. Davidson. 1998. *Open Minds to Equality,* 2nd Edition. Boston: Allyn and Bacon.

Slade, Arthur. 2003. *Dust.* Toronto: HarperCollins.

Smith, Frank. 1997. *Reading Without Nonsense.* New York: Teachers College Press.

Spiro, R. J., P. J. Feltovich, M. J. Jacobson, and R. L. Coulson. 1992. "Cognitive Flexibility, Constructivism, and Hypertext: Random Access Instruction for Advanced Knowledge Acquisition in Ill-Structured Domains." In *Constructivism and the Technology of Instruction: A Conversation,* edited by T. M. Duffy and D. H. Jonassen, pp. 57–76. Hillsdale, NJ: Lawrence Erlbaum Associates.

Swartz, Larry. 2002. *The New Dramathemes,* 3rd Edition. Markham, ON: Pembroke.

Tovani, Cris. 2000. *I Read It But I Don't Get It: Comprehension Strategies for Adolescent Learners.* Portland, ME: Stenhouse.

Vanier, Jean. 2002. *Becoming Human.* Richmond Hill: Daybreak Publications.

Vygotsky, L. S. 1962. *Thought and Language.* Cambridge, MA: MIT Press.

Wheatley, Margaret. 1992. *Turning to One Another: Simple Conversations to Restore Hope to the Future.* San Francisco: Barrett/Koehler Publishers.

Index